parenting
in the pew

guiding your children
into the joy of worship

REVISED AND UPDATED

robbie castleman

IVP Books

An imprint of InterVarsity Press
Downers Grove, Illinois

InterVarsity Press
P.O. Box 1400, Downers Grove, IL 60515-1426
World Wide Web: www.ivpress.com
E-mail: email@ivpress.com

InterVarsity Press® is the book-publishing division of InterVarsity Christian Fellowship/USA®, a
movement of students and faculty active on campus at hundreds of universities, colleges and schools
of nursing in the United States of America, and a member movement of the International Fellowship
of Evangelical Students. For information about local and regional activities, write Public Relations
Dept., InterVarsity Christian Fellowship/USA, 6400 Schroeder Rd., P.O. Box 7895, Madison, WI
53707-7895, or visit the IVCF website at <www.intervarsity.org>.

All Scripture quotations, unless otherwise indicated, are taken from THE HOLY BIBLE, NEW
INTERNATIONAL VERSION®, NIV® Copyright © 1973, 1978, 1984, 2011 by Biblica, Inc.™ Used
by permission. All rights reserved worldwide.

While all stories in this book are true, some names and identifying information in this book have
been changed to protect the privacy of the individuals involved.

Cover design: Cindy Kiple
Images: Tim Nyberg

ISBN 978-0-8308-3777-9

Printed in the United States of America ∞

Library of Congress Cataloging-in-Publication Data

Castleman, Robbie, 1949-
  Parenting in the pew : guiding your children into the joy of worship / Robbie Castleman.—3rd ed.
    pages cm
  ISBN 978-0-8308-3777-9 (pbk. : alk. paper)
  1. Children in public worship. 2. Worship (Religious education) 3. Parenting—Religious
aspects—Christianity. I. Title.
  BV26.2.C37 2013
  249--dc23
                                                                                        2012041097

P	18	17	16	15	14	13	12	11	10	9	8	7	6	5	4	3	2
Y	28	27	26	25	24	23	22	21	20	19	18	17	16	15	14		

dedication

For my children's children
Tyler, Ebenezer, and Tate,
Anastasia, and Zoe

Psalm 103:17

contents

foreword

this is a practical, delightful book, full of innovative ideas coupled with sound theology and spiced with irrepressible humor.

I only wish I'd had it when our children were small. Still, reading it as a great-grandmother has done me good.

By the way, Robbie's mother-in-law came to China years ago. Three missionary families hired her to teach their children. Lucy Fletcher had a profound impact on me just as I was beginning my spiritual pilgrimage. And that influence has been with me all through my life.

Enjoy this book, as I have, and you will be a better parent and a more committed Christian (without realizing it). You will be won over by Robbie's style, spontaneous humor and wise counsel.

Ruth Bell Graham
Montreat, North Carolina, 1993

preface to the revised and updated edition

i get mail. Lots of mail. Lots of mail from wonderful parents and pastors.

A parent and a worship deacon at a small church in Australia wrote, "Thank you so much for writing your book *Parenting in the Pew*! It has had a profound impact on how I view children and worship. It brought together many things I have felt, but not really been able to articulate over the years, both as a child myself and recently as I have become a parent. As a result of this (among other things), the children's ministry at our church has been significantly restructured over the last year."

And this note from a good ol' Google search: "I am not sure if you are the Robbie Castleman who wrote the book *Parenting in the Pew*, but if you are I would like to thank you for your help. . . . I received this book when I visited R. C. Sproul's church 5 or 6 years ago, but just remembered I had it and decided to read it. I started reading last night and could not put it down. My 2.5-year-old sat with me in our worship service today, and it was such a joy to see him watching and learning to worship with us. Our Sunday morning was still a bit chaotic, but I am hopeful that my future diligence in preparation for Sunday will bear fruit."

And here is one note from a pastor who helped guide his congregation through a big change. After I did a worship seminar for the congregation, they eliminated a worship service that ran concurrently with the Sunday school hour so that families could all be together in the sanctuary, as well as participate in age-specific Christian education classes. "Robbie, I recently did a little attendance analysis, and since *Parenting in the Pew* we've seen an 88% increase in children's worship attendance. Not only that, but Adult Education attendance has doubled. God is good!"

Oh, dear Google friends, down-under friends, congregational pastors and children's ministry workers, what a joy to hear from you, write back to you, pray for you and occasionally visit your congregations face-to-face. *Parenting in the Pew* was always "just" a little boy's lunch, just five loaves and two fish, and I continue to be grateful that, by God's grace, it has actually "fed" so many people through the years.

In this third edition of *Parenting in the Pew*, I have enhanced the discussion guide for parent groups and congregations. People have already found the guide very helpful and easy to use. The appendices from the expanded edition have been incorporated into the body of the book as appropriate. I've updated a few illustrations for today's parents, but basically the content and its challenge have not changed. I've found it delightful to include more illustrations, stories and ideas from parents, children's ministry directors, congregations, pastors and children in the book too.

People ask me all the time, "So, how did those two boys of yours turn out?" It is the deepest grace of God in my life that both our sons still love Jesus, love his church and are not afraid to bear witness in the "real world" to the gospel. Our elder son is an artist (with an MFA from the School of the Art Institute of Chicago) and delights to "think theologically" with other artists about life, meaning, beauty, order, truth. Our younger son is a pastor (with an MDiv from Princeton Theological Seminary) who delights to "think theologically" with anyone who crosses his path about life, meaning, beauty, order, truth.

Robert (who now goes by his middle name, Dayton) and Scott have become what I always prayed: men of God who don't play it safe but follow Jesus radically and passionately—imperfectly like all of us, but faithfully. With our answer-to-prayer daughters-in-love, Karen and Rebecca, our grand next generation is being parented in the pew. Tyler, Ebenezer, Anastasia, Tate and Zoe, this edition is for you, your friends and their parents. This is my hope for the new edition of this book—that the church of Jesus Christ will continue to grow intergenerational communities of people learning to worship the God whose steadfast love never ends.

1

daddy, i'd like you to meet my children

I wish I'd paid more attention to the significant moments of my life. I don't remember what my husband was wearing when I met him. I do remember where and when it happened, but I don't remember anything he said. What were his first words to me?

Of course I didn't know that humid evening in New Orleans would change the course of my life. I was in that city to see the French Quarter, not to fall in love. I was distracted by the excitement, the noise, the glitter and the yummy aromas of the Crescent City. I should have paid attention to that interesting young man, but I didn't.

I don't remember the first time my dad saw his first grandchild, my son Robert. Mom flew out two weeks after Robert was born, but it was five months later that Daddy saw and held his grandson. I don't remember how it happened, because we were in the middle of a family wedding. The hubbub of dresses, flowers, shopping sprees, food, rehearsals and the reception grabbed all my attention. There were really important parts of that visit home that were lost to me.

All of us find it easy to miss the truly important moments of life. Distraction, busyness and the clamor of worry about future things rob us of what God may be up to in the present moment of our lives. We usually see the significant minutes, the turning points of our lives, from a distance. Then we pause in wonder and mutter, "Ahh, little did I realize how important that was at the time."

The lives of children are affected by moments that hardly get our attention. Given an adult's confidence and familiarity with the world, it is easy to overlook the often poignant perspective of children. I also learned the value of just quietly watching my children from a distance to see how they deal with people, things, situations and themselves.

As three and four year olds, our boys went twice a week for half a morning to a preschool across the street from our church. The window of our church kitchen provided a view of the preschool playground. Several times a month, I would stand at the window and watch Robert and Scott and pray for insight into who they were "out there" without me and who they would be in the years to come. I'd watch for signs of their emerging gifts and personalities, how they played, defended themselves, recovered from falls and handled themselves when alone.

I was fascinated with how our elder son always had a project of his own. Robert was perfectly content to stack things against a fence by himself or, it seemed to me, play in an imaginary space that only he could envision and take delight in. Other children or his brother could join him or not, but if they did, he was in charge. Scott, on the other hand, had to have people, lots of people. He never seemed to plan anything alone, and I don't think I ever saw him play by himself. In fact, if he saw a child alone, he often went over to them and offered to include them in the game he was helping organize or the adventure that was brewing.

I'm so glad I didn't miss seeing how their later interests were simply an extension of who they always were. I am so glad I lingered at that kitchen window, even though I always had "so much to do" on those "free" mornings. Looking back, I realize the value of seeing what God was doing across the street in my two very different sons and their preschool personalities. It's made it easier to trust God with their uncertain futures, because they are indeed the unique handiwork of God from the get-go.

Paying Attention Pays Off

Paying attention is not always easy for even the most well-intentioned parents. Sometimes I just wanted to unplug the chatterbox. I remember one time making this statement to my toddlers. The chatterbox one calmly proceeded to inform me that he couldn't be unplugged because he had batteries.

It is especially hard to pay attention to children when there is something else to pay attention to. Being immersed in a favorite TV show, an important phone call or a good book in a quiet corner seems to be a signal for children who suddenly find they need attention. The minute you settle on the couch to relax with a magazine, a teenager who hasn't spoken since last week will suddenly want to tell you all about gym class. And isn't it a wonder how the baby always needs to nurse just as Mom sits down to dinner?

Worship can be one of the times when we parents would like to pay attention to something other than our children. Kids can be distracting, aggravating and embarrassing in church. Parenthood can make sitting in a pew a lot of work. Paying attention to our children can make us less attentive to the service.

The temptations to just stay home, or at least to keep the kids out of the sanctuary, are real. It's hard to pay attention to

God and children at the same time.

Training children to pay attention to God, however, is one rare way to have your cake and eat it too. Parenting in the pew can help children and parents pay attention to what is really important.

Learning to pay attention to my children has helped me pay attention to my heavenly Father in worship. And I do remember times when my children were first held in the Father's arms. I can still see Scott's tears offered in repentance as he confessed his "grubby heart" to Jesus. I can still hear "Jesus Christ, the Crucified" boomed loudly and off-key from my toddler sons when they learned this refrain from an old hymn.

I was with them when they first understood a gospel illustration. I answered their questions about a five-syllable word used in a sermon. I was next to Robert and Scott the first time they held the sacred symbols of Christ's body and blood in their hands. I paid attention. These moments of grace and worship are remembered. And treasured.

Training your children to worship is one way to pay attention to the truly important and life-changing moments of life. Parenting in the pew keeps you focused on the significance of the moment, so it is not lost in the distractions of the day.

Training children to worship can allow parents as well as children to pay attention to what God is doing. Parenting in the pew helps you pay attention to the most important thing you can ever train your child to do: worship. Worship is the one very important thing we actually get to do forever.

For many parents, sixty minutes in a pew with a squirmy toddler or a sulky teen can seem like forever. Worship can be the furthest thing from our minds when children are distracting.

Actually, training children to worship is hard for some of us because we ourselves did not have the experience of worshiping as children. Maybe your memories of church in childhood are similar to mine.

Petticoats and Passing Notes

I went to church as a youngster, usually in shiny shoes and an itchy petticoat. I was fairly good and reasonably quiet—at least my body was. Mentally and emotionally I romped outside, counted bricks and made up wild stories about the people in front of me. Eventually, though, I grew tired of counting bricks and doodling in the bulletin and graduated to the "teen balcony" to pass notes and gossip about the people down below.

I was a Sunday-morning dropout in my late teens, contributing to a documented trend noted in church-attendance studies. One reason for quitting was that I had never been trained to worship. I had only been told to be quiet in church.

During my childhood, my dear parents did not know the difference. Mama and Daddy did the best they could with what they knew. Mama grew up "going to church," but not to worship, while Daddy had not gone to church for any reason as a youngster.

During the early years of my childhood, my parents grieved deeply over the loss of their first child, a brother I have never known, to "crib death" (sudden infant death syndrome). Then, when I was four, we were involved in a car accident. Some people who were kind and helpful at the scene of the accident became our friends, and it was they who encouraged my parents to begin attending church and Sunday school. My mother looks back now and muses, "We knew we needed something in our lives." So we went.

As I sat by them, the difference between "going to church" and "going to worship" was something they were just beginning to discover. All I was taught was to "be quiet and be good."

"Be still, and know that I am God" is more biblical (Psalm

46:10). This verse begins to define the difference between "going to church" and "going to worship." Going to worship requires a life transformation and happens out of a new heart, not an old habit. Going to church can be nothing more than smart time management with good intentions. It may not have much at all to do with *worship*.

Just Going to Church

We can just go to church because it is good for us, benefits us, puts our week right, keeps our kids off drugs—and because we like the music. We can settle for going to church because it is "good for us." Giving God attention in worship may seldom influence our thinking or touch our hearts.

On more than a few occasions (usually in a ballpark or a gymnasium) I have overheard the same conversation. It goes something like this:

AMY: You know, now that the kids are bigger, we really do need to get back to church. I think it would do us some good.

CHRISTINA: Yeah, I don't know what we'd do without our church. It keeps the kids busy. They always have something to do.

AMY: Well, Buddy isn't much for a long service. Where do you go?

CHRISTINA: Oh, you'd like our church. It's got some life to it. The music is terrific. Wayne and I like the sermons. They don't go on and on.

AMY: Maybe we'll visit some Sunday. Which church is it?

CHRISTINA: It's Riverside Fellowship. The one with the big stained-glass window and all glass on one side. On the corner of Hyde and Central.

AMY: Oh, I know the one. The daughter of one of the women in our office got married there. It was real nice.

CHRISTINA: I like it. Now that the kids are old enough to sit with their friends, I can just sit back and relax some.

AMY: Well, that's why we've waited to get back to church. It was just too much hassle when the kids were little, but I think it will do them some good now that they are older.

Why do we go to church? My parents took me because none of us were killed in a car wreck when I was four years old. They had made a promise to God.

Some people go because they promised parents or grandparents. Some people, politicians included, go because it's good for image or business. Some people like the "sameness" of church because the world is complicated and even threatening. Lots of people like going to church to get some help and support from others or just to feel better about themselves and life in general. But I think some folks are like Amy and Christina and the old why-to-eat-oatmeal commercial, "It's the right thing to do."

And it is. *Worship,* however, is the rightest of reasons. But worship doesn't come naturally for us humans. God had to train the nation of Israel to worship. He went to great lengths to teach his people how he deserved to be honored and loved and known.

God outlined general guidelines ("Be still . . .") and specific rules ("With a ram prepare a grain offering of two-tenths of an ephah of the finest flour mixed with a third . . ." Numbers 15:6) for his worship. Thus God began with Israel to train a people how to worship him "in the Spirit and in truth" (John 4:24).

God desires our worship. He commands it. His Word trains us in how to love him, how to worship him. The children of

Israel, we and our children must be trained to worship. I've learned along the way and in my study of Scripture that biblical worship is partly intended to help God's people remember, rehearse and reenact God's great story of salvation. To enter into that story week after week with one's children is a great reminder of our place in that story. It's good for us to realize that we *not* the "star" of God's story, but that God is the ultimate means and ends for faith and life—for ourselves and our children. As a mother, I can only stand at a window for thirty minutes during play time, but the Father, who neither slumbers nor sleeps, numbers all our days and watches with a higher wisdom and deeper love than any parent ever could.

Wanted: Training for Worship

Parents teach their children how to make beds, hit baseballs, figure fractions and shop wisely. There are shelves of books, columns of advice and lots of good reasons for developing those skills.

But though we have plenty of advice for finances and child rearing, very little has been written about training children to worship. In *Dr. Dobson Answers Your Questions*, James Dobson affirms that "spiritual training" is important, and he says that the first seven years of a child's life are "prime time" for this training. He provides a twenty-eight-point checklist of questions for parents.

The two checklist questions concerning church/worship are as follows:

- *Is he learning to behave properly in church—God's house?*
- *Is he learning to keep the Lord's Day holy?*

These are two good questions. Parents need help as they try to teach their children about church. But the help they give must train children to worship, not just lessen the stress of an hour in the pew.

Parenting in the Pew is written to help parents train children in the only "proper behavior" for church: worship! This book is an expression of my joy in learning with my children how to remember the Lord's Day and keep it holy.

Parenting in the pew can be a hot battle or a holy triumph of grace. It can consist of whispered commands: "Be quiet," "Shhhhh," "Sit still," or it can contain the most intimate moments of life with God's family together in his presence. Sunday morning with children in the pew can be the longest hour of the week, or it can provide the very best preparation for eternal joy.

Teaching your children to worship—parenting in the pew— is entering the house of your heavenly Father and saying, "Daddy, I'd like you to meet my children." Worship is seeing your Father's smile.

2

worship bc and ad

there is a big difference between worship BC and worship AD—worship "before children" and worship "after diapers." I have heard more than a few parents confess, "I used to get more out of church before I had kids."

But the bigger issue is, What does God get out of worship?

Worship is good for God. Worship concerns itself with God's pleasure, his benefit, his good. Worship is the exercise of our souls in blessing God. In the psalms we read or sing, "Bless the Lord, O my soul." However, our chief concern is usually "Bless my soul, O Lord!"

Encountering the Lord. Meeting Jesus. Hearing his voice. Knowing God. These expectations of worship are met in hearts that are intent on his blessing. But the Lord's benefit is too seldom the desire of our hearts, the work of our souls, the focus of our attention.

We sing, "Breathe on me, breath of God," but what would we do if he did? We pray, "Come, Holy Spirit," but don't prepare for his visitation. We harmonize beautifully "Spirit of the living God, fall afresh on me," but never expect anything new. "When we've been there ten thousand years" can seem like anything but "amazing grace" if we just go to church rather than to worship. And this holds true BC *or* AD.

Children can infringe on our worship experience. I know more than a few parents who have resented the distractions ushered into the pew by the presence of their children. Many just give up. However, children do not have to interfere with *God's* experience of worship. Worship is first a blessing to God, and he values the presence and praise of children (Matthew 18:14; Mark 10:14; Luke 18:16).

The Meaning of Worship

Worship is not a refueling to get us through another week. Worship is not a system of traditions built up over many years of congregational life until everyone feels comfortable. Worship is not a time to unwind, relax, tune out or take a mental vacation.

Worship is not an hour of Christian entertainment. It is not what makes us good people, faithful Christians or successful parents. Worship is not designed as a commodity to sell or a storefront window to attract "shoppers" to come on in for a great selection of congregational programs.

Worship is the surrender of our souls to a God who is jealous for our attention, time and love. Worship is a challenge. With children, it is a *bigger* challenge.

Os Guinness, in his book *Fit Bodies, Fat Minds*, writes that modern people

- worship their work,
- work at their play
- and play at their worship. (Grand Rapids: Baker, 1994)

We need to work at our worship. With children, we often have to work harder. It is interesting to note that some congregations today advertise the time of worship as a "worship experience," not a "worship service." This distinction can communicate a lot about how a congregation thinks about what worship is. If worship is all about our "experience," then to work at worship, especially with young children, can seem like a threat to what you hope is a "great experience." The idea of "service" may indicate to tired parents that worship is one more chore on a to-do list that is already too long.

However, it may come as a surprise to know that in the Hebrew language the word for "service" is the same word used for "worship." It may be good to remind ourselves what we often tell our kids and ourselves from time to time, especially in athletic endeavors: "No guts? No glory!"

Baseball and ballet are taught through participation, practice and patience. Children learn best by doing. Great baseball players are not made in the bleachers. Dancing is not learned by remote control. Children learn to worship by worshiping—through participation, practice and patience.

The task can be overwhelming if you take it seriously. Training children to worship is a zenith of sacred trust. Unlike baseball or ballet, however, worship is best taught by parents, not "professionals."

Worship, ballet and baseball are all learning by example as well. A good trainer or teacher can hit the ball or demonstrate a pirouette. And parents in the pew can show by example what it means to be encountered by God, to love his Son and to respond to the Holy Spirit in worship. Children learn that prayer is important when they see their parents make it a priority. Children learn to give generously when their parents do. Children dress, sing and participate by following examples as well as instruction. When worship is an obvious joy to parents, children will expect to experience the same.

And the trainer can even be a single parent in the pew. On

Sunday mornings, I was the only parent in the pew. My husband is the pastor, so he works every Sunday and can't sit with us. Believe me, with those boys only seventeen months apart in age, I would have appreciated two extra hands at times.

In the pew, I was the worship trainer for our family. And Robert and Scott, now grown, seem to think that I did just fine. Their memories, of both successes and failures, are in this book. Step by step, we learned how to participate. We practiced. And practiced. And practiced.

I have learned to be patient in times of discouragement, spiritual dryness and distraction. I just kept at it. I haven't always done things the way I wanted to. In the early years, training my children to worship was lonely. I didn't know anyone else who was doing the things I was doing with my boys. I wondered at times whether the effort would really make a difference.

And then a few parents began to notice the difference training was making in the pew. My friends asked me, "What are you doing? How do you do it? Why do you do it?" It got easier when these friends began to train their children too. I was encouraged to see the difference that others saw in Rob and Scott. I began to realize that the boys were learning to worship a God they loved.

I made worship training important because I wanted my sons to know God and love him. I didn't want to raise hypocrites, but holy men. I wanted my sons to love the church the way their father does. I wanted their journey of faith to be a bit wiser than mine.

A Question of Motivation

I'll tell you my story so that you can understand my motivation for worship. Sharing my struggle may encourage your own efforts to train your children to worship. If you don't have a deep motivation, an unshakable reason, for training your children to worship, participation will be hollow, practice will be inconsistent, and patience will be nonexistent.

I wasn't always patient. I hated pews. I hated being told when to stand up and sit down, when to bow my head. I hated church bulletins. After all, why did anybody need one? It was the same order week after week after week after week. I hated routine and ritual. I hated "church"!

But there I was—sitting on a hard pew with a redundant bulletin, ready to stand up when signaled. Why? Because I had married the pastor.

Actually, my husband was just about the only thing I didn't hate that first year in the hot, humid, flat South. I was a mountain girl, used to snow skiing and sweaters. What was I doing six feet below sea level in New Orleans, sweating in a sundress?

I didn't belong to this by-the-bulletin bunch. I had come to Jesus in the late sixties, during my junior year in college. I was thrilled with the new way of life God had given me. For two years I had celebrated my new faith sitting on the grass in a park, singing freely, worshiping spontaneously and growing deeply in the rich soil of Scripture. What was I doing married to a Presbyterian minister who actually wore a suit and tie— and only brown, black or dark-blue socks?

Unfettered spontaneity had been the characteristic of my faith that had endeared me to my husband, but I felt as if I were being robbed of my ability to worship God. After one particularly by-the-bulletin Sunday, I was tearful, homesick and ready to scream in frustration. I decided I needed some sympathy. I needed to talk to someone who understood me and knew of my former style of worship and way of life.

So I called my friend Jene in California. I just knew my friend would verbally pat me on the back and say, "There, there, isn't it just awful the way those Presbyterians do things?" Jene had been my Bible teacher and had always helped me see the truth. My Bible teacher would understand!

Jene did and simply said, "There is no external circumstance that can keep you from worship." With greater wisdom than sympathy, Jene made *the* point: *I was the problem in the pew.* Jene reminded me that if the followers of Jesus could worship in chains, in hiding, in sickness, in jungles (without air conditioning), in prison or in peril, I could learn to worship in a pew with my shoes on.

Gradually I learned important lessons about worship. When I struggled in church, it was not the place or the pew that was the source of my distress. A bulletin was not the reason for the dryness of my soul. I had been spiritually thirsty because I had not understood the purpose of worship.

Worship was for God's glory, not my benefit. Although it was a good lesson, it was not an easy one to learn. I had to ask myself, did I truly love God just for himself?

I began to learn that I didn't love God as he deserved. I did love what he had done for me. I loved God so I could feel better. I had loved God easily when the snow sparkled on the ski trail, when jeans-clad, barefooted friends threw away their dope to follow Jesus and when the believers around me were just like me. I had to admit that I loved God when he satisfied my desires.

The question became, Could I meet God's desire for worship? The answer did not come quickly. It came in a Sunday-after-Sunday process. I had to practice. I had to rethink and retrain and repent. But I began to discover God's desire for worship the very next Sunday after Jene's loving rebuke. That Sunday I did not go to church; I went to *worship*. And week after week thereafter, I worked to make the service a part of my heart's offering to God.

Since then I have learned that worship begins in the heart of the believer, with or without a bulletin. With or without shoes. With or without music that suits my taste. With or without stained glass, pews or grass. And with or without children. For eventually I learned, too, that I could worship with children and teach them to worship with me.

The Challenge of Worship

The challenge of worship is to sense yourself more fully in God's presence, to sit at the feet of Jesus with the people of God, to anoint his head with the "oil of joy" (Hebrews 1:9), to bring him a "sacrifice of praise" (Hebrews 13:15). Worship means that for a time all else is set aside to be with Jesus, the Bridegroom of the church—to be together with him. To be alive in his presence.

To do this, and to give our children a sense of this passion, is to worship the Lord "in spirit and truth." A great deal of parenting in the pew is letting our children see us celebrate before the Lord. King David once taught the nation of Israel what it means to worship: "I will celebrate before the LORD. I will become even more undignified than this, and I will be humiliated in my own eyes" (2 Samuel 6:21-22).

It is not a simple thing to be humiliated in your own eyes and to be before the Lord alone. A toddler can certainly contribute to the humble part, but also can make it very difficult to concentrate on being with the Lord. But if our hearts are fixed on being with our children before the *Lord* and not before the congregation, we will begin to experience great relief and freedom.

We can be freed to help our children worship without the pull of external distractions or the self-consciousness of wondering what others are thinking. We can overcome the question that bothers so many parents with children in the pew: What do people think of *me* because of the way my children behave?

Joy is the last word many parents would choose to describe what it's like to sit in a pew with their children. Resentment and frustration are not uncommon feelings for people who "before we had kids" experienced an hour of peace and calm in the pew. Parenting in the pew can be a hassle. Or it can be holy. It depends on who we are and how we see ourselves. Do we sit with our children "in church" or "in worship"?

Too many adults who learned how to be quiet in church are still doing just that. And many of them are passing this along to their children. A family can learn to sit still very well, but be unmoved by the holy presence of God.

God invites families to "be still and know" him. Jesus desires the praise and worship of children. He delights in the songs of infants. God calls us to worship him; he *commands* it. In fact, so serious is this to him that if we humans fail to worship, rocks may take our places.

> When [Jesus] came near the place where the road goes down the Mount of Olives, the whole crowd of disciples began joyfully to praise God in loud voices. . . . Some of the Pharisees in the crowd said to Jesus, "Teacher, rebuke your disciples!"
>
> "I tell you," he replied, "if they keep quiet, the stones will cry out." (Luke 19:37-40)

Parenting in the pew is the process of putting a few rocks out of work.

3

praise and puppies

In the imaginations of youngsters, doctors live in hospitals and teachers live at school. And more than a few children in our years of ministry have been surprised to see my husband at places other than the church building. I remember being in the supermarket one day when we came upon a mother and son from our congregation. The kindergartner whispered to his mom in a voice full of wonder, "Mom! Mr. Breck gets his groceries here too!"

Children identify people with places in rather concrete ways. Sometimes ideas get mixed up with amusing results. My husband "looks like Jesus." And if there is a play, Breck gets to be Jesus, because he is tall, thin and bearded, and has rather shaggy curly hair. Add to this my husband's gentle nature and deep kindness, and one can understand how a child could be confused. One morning three-year-old Matthew waited in the pew for Breck to enter the sanctuary. But we were gone on vacation, and the visiting pastor entered instead. He was a godly man, I am sure, but he was short and balding and had no beard. Matthew was disappointed, to say the least. I wish I could have been there to see this toddler stand up on the pew, stomp his foot and ask loudly, "Well, where's Jesus?"

Matthew just expected Jesus to be at church, and the pictures in his Bible and Sunday-school papers sure looked a lot like the fellow who talked about God every week. It was a delight to hear this story and to see Breck, the very next week, take Matthew in his office for a chat. Breck's stock probably dropped some after that, but the Lord was pleased. God delights in children, in their expectancy, in their vulnerability and in their ability to believe.

These are gifts of grace that children bring to a church family. Parenting in the pew encourages children to participate in the life of the church, to share these gifts of unfettered faith and expectation. Children can enhance the worship of God for the whole congregation.

Children Believe

Children are a symbol of the kingdom, indeed the "greatest" in the kingdom. Matthew recorded,

> At that time the disciples came to Jesus and asked, "Who, then, is the greatest in the kingdom of heaven?"
>
> He called a little child to him, and placed the child among them. And he said: "Truly I tell you, unless you change and become like little children, you will never enter the kingdom of heaven. Therefore, whoever takes the lowly position of this child is the greatest in the kingdom of heaven. And whoever welcomes one such child in my name welcomes me." (Matthew 18:1-5)

We need children in our churches. They can remind us vividly of what it means to be great believers. Young children have the capacity to accept as truth what is told to them by adults. Even at fairly early ages they can learn to tell the difference between the

imaginary and the real if this distinction is made by trusted
adults. But children delight in believing what adults find difficult
to swallow. The ideas of faith need careful telling.

Jesus used the idea of the unseen wind to illustrate the reality of the Spirit. The adult Nicodemus in John's third chapter
needed such an illustration to help him grasp the truth.
Children also find stories, illustrations and word pictures
helpful for grasping ideas of faith that cannot be apprehended
with the five senses.

Children are willing to believe, and this means that their
hearts have a great capacity for worship. Young children desire
to "see" Jesus, to love him, to be with him. More than a few
parents have had to deal with questions about dying after a
description of heaven as the place "where Jesus lives."

I remember our oldest urgently telling my husband to "pull
over!" after one such discussion in our car. With its constant
heavy traffic, Claiborne Avenue in New Orleans is no street to
pull over on. Well, that was four-year-old Robert's point: "We
could all hold hands and lie down in the street and go see
Jesus together!"

This same son asked about our obvious grief over the death
of a teenager in our youth group. Leukemia had claimed Tim's
life about a week before Christmas. When we told Robert of
Tim's death, our toddler jumped up and down with joy and
envy. We asked if he had understood what we meant. Robert
replied with wide-eyed wonder, "Oh, Tim is so happy! He gets
to see Jesus blow out the candles on his birthday cake."

Yes. And Jesus knew that this delightful faith and fervent
love makes for kingdom All-Stars.

Chronological age is important to consider when paying attention to how children think about God and how they learn
to worship. Although individual children are certainly very

different, there are general similarities among children that are very helpful to bear in mind.

Grade-school children have a more informed and sober approach to faith than preschoolers like Matthew, but they are seldom less willing to believe. They just want to know more.

Older grade-school children have learned that parents and teachers can be wrong, but they still don't expect them to be. Yet they ask questions—lots of questions. Adults need to give careful and truthful answers. Scripture needs to be cited time and again as the resource for many answers.

Children tend to believe what they read. Children of this age group need to see that faith is no fairy tale. They may no longer assume that Jesus lives at church, but they need to be confident that he lived in real history. *Veggie Tales* are delightfully helpful in assisting parents in teaching moral ideas and behavior to children—why to tell the truth, why not to gossip, how to do the right thing—but they can be confusing to children and ultimately counterproductive when dealing with real time and space and people in the Scripture. Abraham, Ruth, King David, Peter, James, John and Paul need to be understood as real people for children. The first impression children have of biblical history, God's story of salvation, should reflect at least some of the reality we want our children to begin to believe and grow to understand.

Teenagers aren't as tough as they seem when it comes to worship. In fact, worship can help them deal with a crucial question of faith: "How do I myself know that all this is true?" Teenagers may borrow their parents' car, but they need to own their own faith. Worship can make all the difference between "borrowed" faith and "owned-for-myself" faith.

Teens want to encounter God. They want to hear God speak back to them when they pray. They want to know about the

faith of others. Teens also want to do something for God.
Worship needs to be a big part of that. Too often teens are told
that mowing the church lawn or tending the church nursery is
all they can do for God. Worship is seldom seen as "serving"
God, even though the hour between eleven and noon is called
the "worship service."

From toddlers to teens, kids have a substantial capacity for
worship. God knows that children are quite ready to believe the
truth. Parents need to ask them to listen to it in worship. We
need to help them listen. And we need to listen to them when
they respond to what they've heard.

Children Respond

Participation in every syllable of the service is of major importance in training children to worship. But remember, sometimes an encounter with God won't look like one at first. God
can surprise us with his presence. And children often are the
leaders in boldly approaching the throne of grace.

Jeremy is a dear friend's middle son. One Sunday Jeremy sat
with my grade-school-aged son and me. Jeremy was four. Barely.
During the responsive reading, he was standing in the pew. As
I had learned to do with toddlers, my arms circled around him
as I held the book for him to see, and I pointed to the words as
the reading progressed.

My arms provided control and support. We were concen-
trating on every word. Even though he was too young to read,
Jeremy followed my finger as it pointed to the black words said
by the pastor and the red words recited by the congregation.
We were reflecting together on the amazing personal knowledge
God has of each one of us from Psalm 139.

You know when I sit and when I rise. . . .

My frame was not hidden from you
>> when I was made in the secret place. (vv. 2, 15)

Jeremy listened to the words, watching my finger intently.

>> How precious to me are your thoughts, God! (v. 17)

Suddenly Jeremy cried out in an excited whisper, "Aunt Robbie, Aunt Robbie!" (All the children in that church called me "Aunt.") Looking into his sparkling, dark-brown eyes and ecstatic smile, I interrupted my own reading to whisper, "Jeremy, what is it?"

"Aunt Robbie," Jeremy whispered back energetically, "Jesus knows my dog!"

At first I was stumped. He repeated his discovery with great joy. I thought about the psalm the congregation had just concluded, and remembered Jeremy's dog—a fuzzy mongrel named Precious. That was it! I suddenly saw what Jeremy had heard and understood so well.

"How precious to me are your thoughts, O God!" Jeremy had heard the word and made an odd connection, but hadn't missed the point. He was right. The God we were encountering knows our getting up and our lying down. He knows our frame and the length and content of days lived and yet to come. This God surely does know about Jeremy's dog, Precious.

That four-year-old was learning to worship. Jeremy responded to God with the excitement and wonder and joy that David's psalm was intended to provoke in all of us. God knows all about us! If you have a dog, God knows its name.

God was praised that day by Jeremy's joyous discovery. God was worshiped and adored in that bundle of energy. God was blessed because Jeremy was expected to participate in every part of the liturgy. Because he was helped to do so even as a four-year-old. And because he was *there*.

Children's Worship for Seeker Churches

One of the questions I am most frequently asked about children in worship is, "But what can you do when the parents aren't Christians but are just visiting the church as seekers?" For those who have invited their friends to worship, the concern centers around making sure the adults clearly hear the gospel, enter into worship and are not distracted by or self-conscious about their children's behavior. It might even be the first time these children have ever been inside a church. Isn't it better to have a special program for these children so their parents can pay attention?

My response to this valid and thoughtful concern usually begins with another question: What kind of program? My ultimate hope is that congregations that do have a "children's church" will, in fact, have "children's *worship*" training. Any time developed for children as an option during the worship service should be used to prepare children to participate in that service. Teaching children biblical liturgy is a wonderful outline for child evangelism. God-centered, liturgical worship contains all the elements of the gospel: God's character and worthiness to be adored and honored, human sinfulness and brokenness, the sufficiency of the work of Jesus in his death and resurrection to bring us forgiveness and new life, and our need to surrender our lives to the lordship of the triune God. Biblical worship is story-shaped worship.

A seeker-intensive church can develop children's worship that communicates the gospel while training children in the liturgical parts of the service. The very pattern of the songs, hymns, creeds, prayers and Scripture that make up the liturgy begins to teach them the gospel. Children's worship is helpful only if it is a time of preparation for the worship practice of the congregation. Children's church, on the other hand, is sometimes an extended babysitter service with cut-and-paste, puzzles and play, with a song at the beginning or a prayer at the end. Developing a helpful children's worship service demands no small investment from the congregation. Teachers and leaders are best recruited from those not parenting in the pew themselves—young couples without children, grandparents, singles and the like. A dependable rotation schedule is a must, and training in the church's liturgy is essential. Pastors, worship leaders and church musicians are usually eager to help with this training.

Creating parameters for participation in the development of children's worship is also important. Children up to about the age of four brought by unchurched seekers and congregation members make a good focus. Several churches around the country that promote parenting in the pew have developed a six-month to year-long program for training children in the liturgy of the congregation. Depending on the size of the class, this can be expanded or duplicated for older children of seekers. Believing parents should be discouraged from using children's worship as an excuse to escape the rigors of being with and training their children in worship.

The space for children's worship should be modeled as closely as possible to the setup in the sanctuary. Hymnbooks, Bibles, candles, bulletins and the like should all be similar to those used by the "big people" to help children get used to these objects and their use. The idea is to look at the liturgy of the church from week to week and, by creative repetition and practice, to help children learn the parts and how and why they fit together. The feedback I get from adults who do this usually reflects with amazement how much *they* learned in the process about *their own* liturgy.

Churched parents, of course, can enhance this training with

practice and repetition at home. The friends of unchurched
seekers can use the explanation of children's worship and the
liturgy to share the gospel with their friends who have children.
One benefit of this training is the examination of a congregation's worship to make sure it really is centered in the gospel
and offered to the Lord with thanksgiving and praise.

The best kind of seeker service is one where unchurched
people feel two things simultaneously: "I don't belong here"
and "I want to belong here." The *mysterium tremendum*, God's
fearful majesty, is off-putting and in-drawing at the same time.
The "throne of Grace" is still a throne, not a rocking chair or
floor pillow. The church is not another club to join. It is the
body of Christ, the presence of the kingdom of God in the
world. What a privilege to invite our friends and their children
to know and worship the King!

Children Belong

In their book *Resident Aliens: Life in the Christian Colony*, Stanley
Hauerwas and William Willimon affirm the wisdom of including children in the worship and work of the kingdom.
Nestled almost parenthetically in their chapter on ethical
conduct in the Christian community is this observation:

> In many of our modern, sophisticated congregations,
> children are often viewed as distractions. We tolerate
> children only to the extent they promise to become "adults"
> like us. Adult members sometimes complain that they
> cannot pay attention to the sermon, they cannot listen to
> the beautiful music, when fidgety children are beside them
> in the pews. "Send them away," many adults say. Create
> "Children's Church" so these distracting children can be
> removed in order that we adults can pay attention.

These professors at Duke University conclude their point by noting,

> Interestingly, Jesus put a child in the center of his disciples, "in the midst of them," in order to help them pay attention. . . . The child was a last-ditch effort by God to help the disciples pay attention to the odd nature of God's kingdom. Few acts of Jesus are more radical, countercultural, than his blessing of children. (Nashville: Abingdon, 1989, p. 96)

Now, it must be acknowledged that some churches have developed children's church for reasons other than sending fidgety children away for an hour. Some churches have it to help prepare children for the adult service and to learn creeds and hymns and the meanings behind rituals. Many churches settle for another version of Sunday school with lessons and activities. Even though I consider the former more useful than the latter, I wouldn't be writing this book if I felt it was best. Churches sometimes develop programs for children because parents are not equipped or willing to train their children in the things of faith.

Children Can Help

Parents are the best people to teach their children what it means to worship God. And I believe that parenting in the pew helps adults as well as their offspring to *pay attention*. Children have wonderful ways of making a point that every preacher dreams his congregation will get. They tend to respond immediately to an idea that grabs their attention.

Pastors of the quietest congregations know the joy of hearing an audible answer to rhetorical questions that punctuate a sermon. One time my husband gave a call to missions in the

Lord's words from Isaiah 6:8: "Whom shall I send? And who will go for us?" He paused for effect, and a first-grader called out, "I'll go if my mom will let me!"

More than a few parents have had to comfort their children when the suffering of Good Friday touched tender hearts. I remember the tears of my boys when they understood Jesus' sacrifice for their sin for the first time. They felt so grieved that it had to be that way. Children remind those of us more familiar with the truths of Scripture how we should respond. They remind us all what it means to marvel at God's grace like those who first received it.

Children help us to pay attention to what God is really saying. The first-grade missionary, whose name I cannot remember, and Jeremy both displayed the deep capacity of children to respond to God, to worship in spirit and truth. They responded to the truth of God with awestruck insight—with *worship*.

God was in church on those Sundays, reminding all of us that he knows everything about us, asking us to go and love the world for his sake. Jeremy and the first-grade missionary responded with eager joy. And I'm sure that Jeremy could reassure what's-his-name that God knows everything and would never forget his name.

4

sunday morning starts
on saturday night

It's a fact: more shoes are lost on Sunday morning than all other days of the week combined. Is "Hurry up!" the Sunday-morning call to worship in your home? Does the pressure of finding shoes, scolding a slow one and settling fights over the newspaper funnies diminish your sense of confidence as a Christian parent? Does your hypocrisy quotient increase as the tension of getting out of the house gives way to a warm "Hello!" for the church people you don't live with?

Are you discouraged by the sibling squabbles in the back seat that dismantle the "neat and tidy" look within seconds? Do you habitually run out of adequate change for the Sunday-school offering? Remember you forgot to practice the memory verse with your grade-schooler? Wish your high-schooler would "look nice" without a fight just once?

Do you wonder more often than you'd admit why Sunday mornings are even included in the Christian life? Why do Sunday mornings seem shorter than Saturday mornings? Why do Saturday nights tend to end later? Do you ever mentally prepare lunch or a grocery list during the last verse of the final song?

In an unabridged dictionary, *worship* comes right after *worn, worn-out, worry, worrywart, worse* and *worsen*. Sometimes on Sunday mornings, worship follows the same sequence. Getting children and young people to the worship place is often as far as we get in helping our offspring to worship. As the church dropout rate of older kids indicates, there has got to be a better way.

Sunday morning should be a time of joyous expectation for a family who loves the Lord. But too often it is a morning riddled with strife and filled with regret. Recently I listened to a group of parents share their frustrations with Sunday mornings. These were parents whose lives are given to Christian ministry— parents steeped in Scripture, parents committed to rearing their children in ways that honor the Lord. Even though I understood, my heart broke as Sunday morning was described as "the worst morning of my week." One mother confessed, "Sometimes I'm relieved to stay home if one of the kids is sick." Another said, "I'm just exhausted by the time I get to church."

As I sat listening, I thought about my two teenage sons. Sunday mornings are some of our best memories. I know how much I miss my sons when they aren't beside me in the pew, as I did when they were in high school and spent a few summers in short-term missions overseas.

I've had some Sundays when all did not go as planned (usually for lack of planning), and I've experienced, on occasion, the weariness my friends were expressing. But for the most part, our Sunday mornings have been times of joy and closeness, not strife and estrangement. What has made the difference?

Working to Worship
There is a way to turn the hearts of our children to worship and

take the *worry* and *worn-out* from the Sunday-morning agenda. The key lies in another, better W word: *work.*

The sanctuary is often described as a place to "just relax and unwind," providing a once-a-week hour of reprieve from the demands of the world. It's no wonder that this hour can also become a reprieve from God's command to worship him. Sometimes even the space where worship happens can be less than helpful for parents who want to work at worship with their children. Just recently I was talking to a father of three young children who worshiped in a congregation different from his own while out of town. Unlike the sanctuary at his home church, with its wooden pews and stained glass, the worship center for this congregation had soft theater seats with cup holders. He mentioned to me that he had to work harder to work at worship in that setting, to not just chill like he does while watching a movie. He went on to comment how much harder it would be to explain the intention of this space to his children, to help them worship and not just "watch."

Worship is work, hard work. It is also rewarding work. To worship the Lord "in spirit and truth" does not come easily, and it certainly does not come naturally to us. It is difficult to worship on the leftover energy of a long week and a late Saturday. But the Sunday-morning encounter with God is worthy of our best energy, not our least.

The Lord of life promises to accompany us in worship. We come upon unexpected stores of energy when we remember that worship is a joyous privilege. God's mighty energy will be at work in us to revitalize our weary spirits. We will find rest for our souls.

Sundays are special. Children know that there is a difference between a birthday cake and an any-day cake. Birthday cakes are planned, designed in a special way and focused on the person being celebrated. A birthday cake is the person's favorite; the frosting is sweeter, and the anticipation is so thick you could cut it with a knife. An any-day cake can be eaten without much introduction, but a birthday cake is eaten after candles and songs and ceremony.

Technically, cake is cake. It's the day, the parents and the preparation that set birthday cakes apart. Birthday cakes are cakes with an attitude!

Worship is loving the Lord with an attitude. We love the Lord every day, but Sunday is God's favorite flavor, and the frosting is sweeter.

Heart Preparation

Preparing a special cake or birthday party begins with a desire in our hearts to give honor on a special day. I know that I have a much better frame of mind on a busy celebration day if I have gone through an attitude check. I need to remember why all of this is worth doing.

Parenting in the pew begins with an attitude check. Are you eager, or are you going through the motions? Are you profoundly grateful for the saving work of Christ on the cross, or are you religious by habit or culture? Are you more conscious of how God sees you in worship than of how others see you in church? Is worship time priority time? Do you talk about preparations for worship during the week? Do your children sense that, just as they look forward to birthdays, you can hardly wait for Sunday to get here?

Parenting in the pew—teaching our children to worship—is a sacrifice of praise and thanksgiving that God rejoices to receive. So how do we begin the practical work of preparing this offering once our attitude is poised on tiptoes of expectancy and love? Well, Sunday morning begins on Saturday night. Our children need to hear us say to friends or baby-sitters, "No, we won't be too late; we are set to worship God tomorrow morning."

Home Preparation

Sunday mornings seem shorter than other mornings because they often start later. For many of us, it's much easier to get up early on Saturday to prepare a picnic than it is to get up early on Sunday to prepare our sacrifice of praise. The call to worship begins with the chime of the alarm clock that is set with honoring the Lord's Day in mind.

Starting with infants, who seem to require an enormous amount of baggage for every contingency, Sundays need to embrace the idea of rest embedded in the Lord's Day. Some of the distress reflected in infant fussiness in the church nursery begins with parental hurry and stress. One way to make the Sunday nursery setting acceptable to your youngest children is to take time upon arrival to linger and share that space with the infant or pre-toddler. This, in turn, is easier if plans are made and all the baby's necessities are packed up early.

With older children, beginning with toddlers, start Sundays with an announcement that the very best day of the week is about to begin. When my boys were small, I set the tone by telling them, "Jesus is excited. This is his special day!"

Not only was this true, but as they got older, the specialness of the day grew with them. One custom was our "Jesus music" on Sunday mornings. It is a little harder to get short-tempered when "Sing Alleluia" lingers in the air.

It is true that Sunday mornings seem more complicated than other mornings. The schedule is different; the entire family may have different responsibilities for the morning at church; and usually all members of the family leave home at the same time. In addition to this, the Christian family must recognize that we have an enemy, one who delights in hypocrisy and distraction. The devil, in all of his evil power, wants to undo the worship we prepare for God. It is no surprise that Sunday morning can be a time of spiritual warfare.

I became aware of this the hard way on a Sunday morning when my boys were both in junior high school—and acting like it. Because junior-high kids know *everything*, they think they can reimagine the way things ought to be. And they may or may not let you know about this brave new world. Well, one Sunday morning I really lost it. "It" means my mouth, my temper and my well-intended hope to act like a mother who actually loves her children no matter what. My anger at their behavior was over-the-top for me, and I wondered, "Where did *that* come from?" From that morning on, I prayed more as I realized there was an enemy more powerful than two (often aggravating) junior-high boys.

Good warriors prepare for the battle and do not encourage the advance of the enemy. God's Word both commands and invites his people to "remember the Sabbath day," the Lord's Day for Christians, and to "keep it holy." Jesus' promise concerning worship in "Spirit and in truth" (John 4:24) pushes against our constant temptation only to keep up appearances, turning God's command and invitation to rest into just one more thing to do. God's grace and our faith on Sunday mornings are needed to win the battle. The exercise of our faith needs to be thoughtful and practical. Sometimes putting on the "full armor of God" (Ephesians 6:10-18) begins with finding a pair of socks that match.

Dressing for Worship
Clothes, shoes and socks for Sunday need to be ready by Saturday evening. Children need to help set the agenda for what to

wear. And kids are different. One child may find it delightful to "wear a tie like Dad" or "shiny shoes like Mom" on Sundays. Another child (same parents, same rearing, same everything) thinks a clean T-shirt without a slogan is more than enough.

One of my childhood memories of Sunday mornings was having to wear stiff dresses I couldn't breathe in, let alone drink punch in, play in or pray in. So I've never had much interest in investing in "Sunday clothes" for my kids or myself. I wanted them to dress for worship, not for me. My older son is Mr. Casual; he wore a tie for the basketball team before he ever wore a tie to church (and didn't like it much then). On the other hand, my younger son enjoys dressing up and likes to "look good" all the time.

I actually believe my husband got a raise once because the church thought our son Scott had only one shirt—his favorite purple one. I think that for an entire year purple was his personal liturgical color. The point is, I never wanted what my children wore to compete for their attention in preparing to encounter God in worship. We allowed them to dress as they liked—as long as it was ready to be worn by Saturday evening.

Too many Sundays are lost with lost socks. Too many Sundays are overshadowed by what we wear and how we look. One question that is helpful for all worshipers to ask is, How does what I wear reflect both my love and my respect for God? Family style may differ on the particulars of how to answer the question, but both a respect for God's holiness and a proper response to God's grace need to be considered when preparing for worship.

Thinking Ahead: A Tithe or a Tip

In addition to advance planning for what to wear, anticipating what the family needs can help return joy to Sunday mornings.

Memory verses can be rehearsed on Saturday. Supplies for
Sunday-school projects can be obtained ahead of time—that is,
if the children happen to remember—before you are pulling
into the church parking lot—that they were supposed to bring
twelve colors of felt for the twelve-tribes-of-Israel display. Remember, we can do only so much, and nothing is foolproof.

Money for the offering is a constant need from Sunday to
Sunday, and this gives parents the opportunity to teach children
an important aspect of faith—Christian obedience. Teaching
children to tithe can be an exciting part of learning to trust
God and to participate in the work of his people.

Begin having children prepare their offering for Sunday at
the earliest age. If your church uses envelopes for this purpose,
it can be helpful for each child in the family to have them.
Usually the envelopes are numbered and provide a place for the
name of the giver, but any kind of envelope will do. Younger
children like to write their names, and this can give them a
greater sense of importance and involvement in their gift.
When they were little, I had the boys "draw a picture for Jesus"
on the outside of the envelope to decorate their offering. Jesus
and the money-counter deacons were thrilled with shark fights,
fighter jet crashes, big bugs, alien monsters and the occasional
Bible scene. There were moments when I thought, *If I only had
a girl, Jesus could get rainbows and flowers and gentle creatures in
the serene bliss of nature.* Sigh.

If your church uses faith pledges for giving, children should
be involved in the process as much as this is appropriate. Preschool children can commit a set amount of money. When
arithmetic days begin, parents can teach the concept of tithing.
Even 10 percent of a two-dollar allowance is important to the
Lord when it is offered in faith and obedience. These two
spiritual gifts are worth far more than twenty cents.

It has been a pleasure to see Rob and Scott grow in their commitment to tithe—from toddlers learning to give Jesus "the shiny penny" to grade-school days when they looked in their wallets each week, figured out what 10 percent was and gave that. Some of this money was left over from the previous week's allowance, which had already been tithed. I wasn't about to clarify that money is usually tithed once.

During their teen years, I became more detached from the process; they figured out their own commitment in giving. They understood that 10 percent is where to begin rather than a goal one hopes to reach eventually. When Rob and Scott were short on money, it was usually because they were behind on their chores or had not been faithful in their giving. Trusting God in the area of finances is an important lesson to learn over a lifetime.

Once one of the boys wanted a pair of special tennis shoes. He knew that if he tithed, the shoes would be financially out of reach. On this occasion he gave a tithe in faith if not in joy. The next week, the shoes he wanted went on sale, and he was able to buy them. As we left the shoe store he commented, "Mom, I think I got these shoes because I tithed. I almost didn't. Wow, now they are really special." (I know this sounds like a scripted comment from an old family sitcom, back when TV mothers all wore pearls, but this is really what my kid said. It blew me away.)

Now, admittedly, anyone can begin to play manipulative games with the theology of tithing. But in this case I think God picked a lesson that would communicate to a fifteen-year-old boy. Shoes are a very big deal to a boy, and faith is a very big deal to God. Learning to put God first and to trust him to provide is no small lesson for anyone.

Teaching children to tithe can help develop a generous attitude about giving praise, time, goods and blessing to God.

Even very young children can be given money to place in the plate or offering envelope. It is good if children can feel that what is given away is something from themselves, not the parent. Toddlers and preschoolers are not often given a set allowance for household chores. If they are given money for the offering then, it should be given to them with a sense of being personally under their charge and keeping. Putting the money in their own pockets or purses lends a sense of possession and special purpose. It is best if this money is given at home on Saturday night or Sunday morning, and not at the last minute.

Too many parents give their kids pocket change to put in the plate, just as they let their children push the buttons in elevators. Not only is this not an offering from the child's resources, but it communicates that God can be honored with spare change we don't really value or need rather than a tithe. Many people end up tipping God with spare change all their lives—and give pretty skimpy tips at that. Children need to learn the joy of generous giving as a part of the family of faith and the community of the church.

It's helpful when children learn this, not just from the generosity of what parents give, but from seeing week after week the joy of the giving itself. Like most people, our family got paid every two weeks, and for years I put our tithe in the plate every two weeks. Even though I knew I was "good with God," I always had a fleeting inkling that I should say on the "off week" to someone near me, "I put in last week when it was payday week." Somehow, not participating in that moment felt funny. Then I heard someone suggest at a seminar that it's helpful for engaging in every movement of worship to split the two-week offering into two checks. Now, why didn't I think of that? So, that's what I did, and this practice made all the difference in how I thought about participating in worship. I think it was this change in me that helped me think of the envelope idea for my boys when they came along. And, even today, when I do most of my banking and bill paying online, I have a physical check made out for every week just to be fully present in the practice of worship with the community of God's people.

Coming to Worship

Children need to sense our excitement about worshiping with God's people. Too many conversations to and from church are filled with complaints and discontent—criticisms of pastors, programs and fellow parishioners. Instead, children need to hear how the Lord met us in worship, how much we learned in Sunday school, what we love about our church family. Our children need to see through our behavior how the Spirit is at work for his purposes in our communities of faith. A heart of gratitude and eyes of faith are easier to have when Sunday is more holy and less hassle.

A family's commitment to weekly worship can also help many other things be less distracting. Helping children develop a stable and worthy fixed center for their lives is invaluable in a culture with exhaustive options. "Over-choice" is a less-than-helpful reality of children who experience burnout from a myriad of things meant to enrich their lives. One challenge for a family's commitment to worship on the Lord's Day is the encroachment of sports on Sunday mornings. This is a bigger challenge in some regions of a country than in others, but the commitment of a family to the primacy of weekly worship communicates something foundationally important for children about the nature of faith and life. Some families belong to a congregation with a variety of times available for worship and others don't, but in either case parents need to underscore the priority of the lordship of Jesus and the importance of acknowledging this in a commitment to worship. Worship cannot be subject to the options of over-choice, like choosing between baseball or piano, ballet or Scouts, if parents want to model part of what it costs to be a follower of Jesus in our world.

In my work with congregations, I've had good conversations with parents concerning making hard choices as a family about "what to do" challenges. These are often not just difficult at the time decisions are made; parents usually don't have any idea of the long-term impact of the decision until years later. However, when a family has a few things that are nonnegotiable in place, decisions in times of pressure can be a bit easier to make stick. And, in the long run, good commitments that help decision making for little things can make a big difference.

I was talking with our son Scott recently about sports conflicts on a Sunday morning, and I asked him if he remembered the day he went to worship wearing his baseball uniform so we could leave straight for the park after the service. His team was in the playoffs, and even though Scott would miss the first game in the morning, we told the coach we'd come right after worship. The coach was not happy to miss his best hitter and first baseman for the morning game, and he didn't start our six-year-old first-grader for the afternoon game.

As parents we understandably fretted a bit over how all this would affect Scott; we worried if he would resent us or even the Lord, and we asked him after the game how he felt about all of it. Scott didn't remember much about this morning in his childhood, so he asked, "What did I say?" I told him what he said, because a mother does ponder things like this. "Well, I felt sorta bad when Coach didn't let me play at first, but Jesus was real proud of me, and that made me feel better." We didn't know what sticking to our guns might mean on that Sunday morning, but after I told him what he said as a six-year-old, Scott commented that this must have been the start of nonnegotiable commitments concerning faith for his family. Parenting is never easy or uncomplicated, but it can be a bit simpler if there a few nonnegotiables at the center.

Simplifying Sundays

I always try to keep Sunday simple. Breakfast is juice and rolls or doughnuts that we don't have other days of the week. I don't prepare a special lunch or leave anything cooking in the oven. We habitually have college students or lonely parishioners over for lunch. Most times we have sandwiches that guests help prepare. Working in the kitchen and helping set the table is more like home to folks than a fancy meal that preoccupied the cook during worship. Often people who fuss less usually practice hospitality more.

Keeping Sunday simple can help keep the day special for God too. We need to recapture God's intention for setting aside time for community worship as a part of the Lord's Day. Jesus said that God's day to "cease" (the literal meaning of *sabbath*) one day in seven would not come naturally for human beings. This day was made for us as a gift from God, but people find it more natural to plan stuff, do stuff and stay busy than to rest (Mark 2:27).

The correct balance comes when we first consider the inward disposition of our hearts. This is what God sees. What makes my heart most ready for worship is what is important. Can dressing special help some children feel how Sunday is special to God? I think for some families, yes, this can help. Simple Sundays and casual clothes help in our home. In a fairly distant second place, we consider the outward appearance that can affect our community. Once people know your heart, however, this is less important; they won't really care what you wear or what you feed them for lunch.

Called to Worship

The call to worship centers on the One who calls us. This call is not a friendly suggestion, but a loving command. God is worthy of our worship. The Lord alone is a worthy recipient of our adoration and praise. He is watchful when we worship.

God sees us. God sees our posture, our faces, our antics in the pew. God knows our hearts and minds. One of the first things I began to impress upon my children was this fact: God is present. He is looking at you, and he cares about how you show him that you love him and that you think he is special.

God sees me. So do my children. I let my kids watch me prepare for worship, sense my anticipation, get ready for God's favorite day. And I have tried to make Sunday morning our favorite time of the week. With few hassles and regrets over one of us "losing it," our Sundays have become a holy joy.

5

counting bricks or encountering god

ask any nine-year-old who goes to church and she can tell you

- *how many bricks there are between the floor and ceiling of the sanctuary*
- *how many red pieces there are in any stained-glass window*
- *how many people in the choir have gray hair or glasses, or don't pray with their eyes shut*

Of course this all depends on the sanctuary structure, but regardless of whether the building is Gothic or gymnasium, kids have counted all sorts of stuff to keep them occupied during worship. (Of course, this is something no parent ever does!)

Why is it that children who refuse to nap all week nod off before the preacher is three sentences into the sermon? Any child can tell you that it takes a lot of energy to sit still and be quiet during church. Most children will also testify that coloring in all the Os in the bulletin is harder than it seems. Especially with all the interruptions for hymns, creeds and offerings.

One of the biggest challenges for parenting in the pew is

training children to pay attention to what is happening—the worship of God—and helping them be a part of it.

Ask adults what they remember about church as a child, and the responses will most often mention the music, the building itself or how hard it was to sit still. A lot of us counted bricks, colored in the Os and daydreamed, or really dreamed, during the sermon.

Adults who recall some spiritual impact "at church" often connect them to services or occasions that were unusual— perhaps a funeral or a revival with a guest speaker or a special service of music. These types of services can make long-lasting impressions on children.

When something in worship is different or unusual, it holds a child's attention longer. This is true for most things in our children's culture. Entertainment has become a standard part of American expectations for education. The creativity of *Sesame Street* and other early-learning programs popularized the idea that we entertain to teach. The generation of young people who learned their ABCs with Big Bird demanded video with their music as they grew into adolescent years. Music videos and MTV grew out of this generational TV experience.

The idea that successful worship is entertaining is not considered outlandish in our culture. *Sesame Street* saints want to be entertained. They expect creativity to hold their attention. Entertainment can be furnished by the service itself or by well-meaning parents who provide coloring books or games to entertain children and keep them quiet during church.

But worship-as-entertainment will not accelerate the spiritual growth of our children. (Educational entertainment has not improved our children's scholastic abilities either.) Worship needs to be the one realm in our culture that refuses to accept the world's addiction to be entertained in order to learn.

This does not preclude creativity or change in worship, but it does mandate that services of worship be designed for God's pleasure, not for our entertainment. At the same time, God's desire does address a child's recognition of spiritual needs and interests.

Children are keenly aware of spiritual needs. They long for forgiveness in the wake of wrongdoing or failure. They know the pain of breaking promises to themselves and to others. The I'll-never-do-that-again variety of repentance is part of every child's experience. Teens go through turbulent times of sorting out personhood issues and questions surrounding the truth of faith. Young people want to know if God is real, if prayer really works, if the stories of Scripture are fact. Children want to know for themselves whether "Jesus loves me" is more than just a song.

When children are trained to worship, when they are helped to develop as spiritually attuned people, they can begin to encounter God in powerful ways. Counting bricks is no match for a God who longs for our attention. Entertainment is no match for worship. Entertainment fills up our time; worship fits us for eternity.

Be with Your Children

Paying attention in worship is foundational to training children in the pew. And giving attention to our children during this time is essential. It is very important that parents and children sit together during worship.

On the surface this seems obvious, but many parents find it a relief to let their grade school and older children sit with friends. Children often ask whether they can sit with their pals. When Rob and Scott asked, they were consistently told the reason they needed to stay with me: "It is much harder to pay attention to God when you want to pay attention to your friend. You will have time later to be with your friend; right now Jesus wants all of our attention because he has something to say to us."

There is no substitute for being with your children. During the junior-high years, I let my children know that they could always ask to sit elsewhere and then blame me for denying their request. Sometimes as parents we have to look pretty mean just to help our kids save face. As high-schoolers, the boys saved me a seat or came through the sanctuary to join me, depending on who got to the sanctuary first after Sunday school.

For parents, being with older teens in worship can seem unimportant. But at this age, training is increasingly transformed into companionship. This can be the time when expressions of worship take on new depth and meaning. It is important for parents to be a part of a teenager's reflections on faith and truth. If the expectation has been communicated in love and in terms of desire rather than denial, teens are cooperative.

Friends are a very important part of teen life. In most churches there are youth-group teens who attend Sunday services without parents. These kids are usually eager to join other teens and their parents in the pew. So Rob and Scott sat with me in worship and their friends joined us.

There may be times when schedules or responsibilities mean that parents and teens do not end up sitting together. But it's best if such times are limited and not allowed to evolve into habitual patterns.

It's true that young people find great security in having rules that don't budge. As Rob and Scott grew up, they simply began to turn down offers to sit away from me, and sometimes they would explain why. More than a few parents of teens have commented on how the boys and I sit together in worship. I treasured the noticeable affection between us that is sometimes unusual for teens and parents.

This companionship has not been won without some cost to my own preferences. For example, I love to sing, but I have rarely been able to participate in the church choir. Many choirs are in the front of the sanctuary, either behind or to the side of the pulpit. Traditionally, the children of the folks who sing in the choir are not included in the seating. Young children do squirm, scratch, stare and point (among a myriad of unmentionables). They can be distracting if seated in a visible area in front of the congregation. When the choir stands to sing, what do the children do then?

The congregation my husband pastored for ten years, where my boys grew from infancy to fifth and sixth grade, allowed children to sit with parents who sang in the choir. The sanctuary had some physical flexibility; at one point the choir was moved from the pulpit area to one side of the sanctuary. This provided a place with less potential for distraction. Such flexibility would have been harder to achieve if the choir loft had been a permanent fixture, as it is in many sanctuaries.

When the choir sang, usually the children sat quietly. Most held hymnbooks, as they had been taught to follow along while parents sang. Most of the children who sat in the choir came to church with only one parent. If both parents attended and only one sang in the choir, the children sat with the other parent in the pew. And grandparents could fill the role of this other training parent if necessary.

Seating children with the choir can be more difficult as children get older, for unless they are included as singing members of the choir, they may not want to sit in the choir section. If the choir loft is in the balcony of a church or in the back, however, I think including children in that seating arrangement poses fewer problems.

Much hinges on the choir director's attitude. If parents in the choir are able to work at training children to worship God, directors should be willing to consider this unorthodox arrangement. Children belong with parents in the pew, and sometimes the pew happens to be in a choir loft.

As children become older and more reticent to sit with the choir, their parents should be free to sit in the congregation and then join the choir for special music. They can sit in an area near the entrance to the loft, and another adult can help children worship during the choir's musical offering to the Lord. In the church where we served during my sons' grade-school years, this arrangement worked because the church was committed to parents teaching their children to worship. I believe the Lord was glorified by this, and we all agreed to be "humiliated in our own eyes" together.

In another congregation, I simply decided to sit with my children in the pew and forgo participation in the choir. The logistics of the loft, the preferences of the director and the ages of the boys all contributed to this decision. I've had regrets at times about not being part of the choir, but I have no doubts that I made the right choice—especially when one of my six-foot sons put his arm around me in worship and helped me pay attention.

Being in the Sanctuary

For several years I have had the opportunity to share ideas on parenting in the pew at seminars. Parents are often concerned about the appropriate ages to include children in all or part of the worship service. I usually offer the following age-related guidelines, though I recognize that children are different and developmental patterns need to be taken into account.

Older infants and toddlers up to two and a half or three years old do well in the nursery and toddler areas. Nursing infants and older toddlers do well in the service about half of the time. Three-year-olds, and some younger children, can be trained to participate in worship that includes the creed, Scripture readings, music and the offering. In most Protestant, evangelical or charismatic congregations, this is a little more than half of a service. By about the fourth year of age, children can be in a service of worship for the entire time.

In our congregation a sermon just for younger children is included after hymns, readings, a choral anthem and the creed. Children are asked to come forward and are taught the main point of the upcoming adult sermon in a shorter, more anecdotal way. Children younger than four are then given time to leave the sanctuary for supervised toddler activities that are designed to teach them a part of the liturgy. This helps them anticipate the time when they are old enough to stay, and it helps prepare them to participate when they do. It's sort of like worship preschool.

Some churches conduct children's church for children well past toddler age. This may or may not include a time of worship. When children older than four leave for their own "church," both these children and their parents can miss a lot. I've been eager to guide my sons in worship and have not wanted to give that privilege away to anyone.

But children's church can be very helpful *if it is designed to train children in worship.* Too many children's churches are cut-and-paste times to keep children occupied until the adult service is over. If children are encouraged to leave the service before the "long parts" and this continues into grade school, it's no wonder that older kids balk or succumb to boredom when they are "too old" and have to stay in the sanctuary for the entire "adult" service.

Parents must put a positive twist on this incredible privilege. In our home, the fourth birthday was an exceptional celebration. This birthday meant being "old enough" to stay in for the whole service. It was a milestone. Worship is a privilege, and most four-year-olds are ready for more. I remember that Scott made the typical second-born request to start early. But he had to wait, and this added to the anticipation and sense of specialness. For a few months after he turned five, Robert felt more elite than ever. After Scott's fourth birthday, it was fun to see his excitement as he remained in the pew after the younger kids went off to children's church. He was finally a "big boy."

Being Attentive

Once you have your children with you in the service, how do you keep them there? How do you keep them there in mind and spirit as well as in body?

Many kids are allowed to leave at all sorts of times during a service of worship. It is amazing how many young people have to go to the bathroom during church. These are often the same youngsters who can play nine innings of baseball without a pit stop.

Bathroom "emergencies" usually occur during the "long parts" of a service. To keep my children out of the potty parade, I did a few simple things. We avoided water-fountain visits between Sunday school and worship. (The attraction of a church water fountain for children is one of life's great mysteries. Water is usually the last thing a kid will drink at home. Maybe they think it's holy water.)

We made a bathroom stop between Sunday school and church. (The aversion kids have for going to the bathroom at logical times is another one of life's mysteries.) The boys knew that going to the bathroom during the worship service was not allowed. Knowing this from the very beginning helped them cooperate about the bathroom visit.

Of course there were exceptions when leaving the sanctuary was allowed. At the sudden onset of a bloody nose or flu symptoms, a parent should accompany the child out to help remedy the situation. Such symptoms are obvious, and every parent knows the difference between the fake and the real thing. It has to do with paleness, clammy hands and what mood the child is in. (It is amazing that these real emergencies occur during the quietest parts of the service, a phenomenon also noticeable with infants who have gas.)

Including children in the worship of God means that some other things need to be excluded. If we want our children to learn to pay attention to the Lord, we will eliminate as many distractions as possible.

This means that toys, loose change, books, paper, pads, pencils, coloring books, dolls, trucks and electronic games should stay at home. It helps children to be empty-handed except when holding the hymnbook to sing, the bulletin when in use or the Bible during the reading of Scripture. Even tracing the travels of Paul on the maps in the back of the Bible is off-limits except during a sermon detailing Paul's missionary journeys. Kids are quick to think of all sorts of diversions, even religious ones, to pass the time in the pew if that's all that's expected of them.

Candy, gum or the like to "keep them quiet" is not helpful either. Training children to worship means that they are asked to pay attention and are helped to do so. Being quiet comes as they learn to listen and worship, not as they are entertained by games and kept quiet with gum.

Naturally, a child who is being trained to worship can be distracted by other children who are allowed to play in the pew.

When Rob and Scott asked why some other children got to color or play with toys in the service, I answered in positive terms about why we were at worship, not in negative terms of why play was not allowed. This helped the boys feel special and not deprived. In general, I always tried to sit away from children who were allowed to have toys and books. As other parents joined me in parenting in the pew, we sat near each other and helped each other out.

Being Quiet

An expectation of paying attention is foundational for learning to worship. Parents sit with their children to help them do this, but there is more to paying attention than mere proximity will provide.

Simply telling children to be quiet is not the way to draw their attention to the worship that is taking place. The purpose of parenting in the pew is to train a child to *worship*, not to be quiet. Quietness at certain times may enhance their ability to worship, but quietness is a means to this effort, not the end.

This distinction is of tremendous importance to a child. It is also a great help to your nerves. It makes sense that when our attention is focused on what is happening in worship, with or without children, our own sense of being in God's presence is enriched. If our children's lack of quietness preoccupies us rather than worship itself, we are simply in the pew in the presence of our kids and are probably feeling far from the presence of God.

But training children to worship does not always enhance our own experience of being before the Lord, especially at first. On a feeling level, the experience of worship may seem impoverished by the demands of parenting in the pew. The number of times children must be helped to concentrate, pay attention and enter into the worship service is almost beyond counting. The effort can be exhausting. And it can be pleasing to God.

It can seem paradoxical that to help a child to develop concentration and a sense of quietness for worship, parents have to talk more. If you sit close to your children, however, you can give whispered instructions and reminders rather easily and with little or no distraction to others.

Where parents sit with children can be important. I always tried to avoid sitting too close to "best friends" when the kids were very young. The temptation of distractions was too great. But it can be very helpful to sit near other parents who are training their children to worship. Such parents can understand whispers, share agendas and help each other out. Worship-training parents and friends can encourage each other and pinch hit for each other as needed. And on a day that goes badly, parents in the pew can remind each other that it's really worth it in the long run.

Helping children pay attention is essential no matter how structured or unstructured a church service may be. All churches have a liturgy. Some are centuries old, some are only as old as a congregation, some are new every Sunday. A liturgy reflects the historical roots of faith as well as a congregation's history and style preference. The point is to encourage our children's participation in worship, using the liturgy in a way that is appropriate for their ages.

It's actually quite easy to see that from a very early age children naturally love liturgies, especially the "liturgy" of bedtime. Very young toddlers often have a bedtime story and very, very often they want the same story. Night after night. Children love knowing what comes next, don't they? And if you are tired and skip a page, these sweet little gremlins catch you every time. I remember thinking if I had to "pat that bunny" one more time, I was going to skin him for dinner.

Helping Children Learn the Rhythm of God's Grace

The help that a learned rhythm offers children in learning about God isn't just about Sunday morning. The whole cycle of God's story that marks many congregational communities can help train children to participate in and understand God's grace in the story of Jesus. The story starts with the season of Advent, which begins the fourth Sunday before Christmas. Families can use Advent calendars, wreaths and family devotional times to help children anticipate the arrival of Jesus' birthday.

Sometimes, of course, this wonderful effort can backfire on you. A young couple in our congregation told me about their four-year-old and his joy in opening a little window every day in their Advent calendar. One night this little guy made a quasi-spiritual comment, and Dad jumped right into a conversation about the comment. He ended by asking if his son would like to "ask Jesus to live in your heart." This four-year-old looked at his dad as if he was out of his mind and said, "Well, Daddy, how can I? Jesus isn't even born yet!"

The Advent and Christmas season ends on Epiphany, which is January 6, and is celebrated on the Sunday after that date. Epiphany is all about God showing the world who Jesus is and brings together three stories of the faith: the visitation of the wise men, the baptism of Jesus by John and Jesus' first sign of hidden glory, turning water into wine. The next season of the story is Lent, approximately the forty days before Easter, which is a time to think about human sin and brokenness and our need for a Savior. The journey to the cross and the death of Jesus can deeply touch children, and they get their need for forgiveness with surprisingly clarity.

I'll never forget the Holy Thursday service when our boys were about five and six years of age. As the Gospel passages were read, the lights in the sanctuary were dimmed slowly and candles were snuffed to help the congregation reflect on the suffering and death of Jesus as the Light of the World. Suddenly our younger son started crying. Loudly. Big heaving sobs. I thought his appendix had burst. I turned and said, "What's the matter?" He simply confessed, "I am, Mama. I'm the reason Jesus had to die." What a precious moment to share how this bad news about us leads to a Friday that was good for us and shows how much God loves us.

A few people sitting near us heard all of this, and it wasn't long until gentle crying and lots of sniffing were heard throughout the sanctuary. And rightly so. This young worshiper heard the story with fresh ears and a tender heart. As I reflected on this later, I thought, why don't we all cry every time? It was good to cry. It makes the Easter victory all the more precious.

Easter season is the next "beat" in the rhythm of the Christian story, and it often begins with an early Sunday-morning service outdoors when the congregation is reminded of that first journey to the garden and the surprise that the tomb was empty. Christ is risen! He is risen indeed! The Easter season continues for several weeks that mark the bodily ascension of Jesus and the sending of the Holy Spirit at Pentecost. It often ends on Trinity Sunday, the Sunday following Pentecost. The rhythm of redemption's story has brought the congregation to early summer, and by late autumn the story begins again.

When parents read a good story to their children, the cry after the last page is often, "Read it again!" The story of salvation is the church's story of God's grace and different congregations go about telling the story in a variety of ways. Some congregations change banners hanging in the sanctuary from season to season. Many traditional congregations change the color of the clothes on the pulpit and communion table, and the collars on choir robes too. I have a friend who directs children's ministries for her congregation who told me she once asked kindergarteners what their favorite holiday was. She said one five-year-old responded with enthusiasm that his favorite one was "the red one!" (Red is the traditional color of Pentecost.) She asked him why, and he responded, "It's the birthday of the church, and I love birthdays."

Church art, changes in colors, noting the season of the story in children's sermons, the use of an Advent wreath in worship can all help children catch the rhythm of the story of salvation year after year, Sunday after Sunday. This is the "old, old story" that children hear for the first time; no wonder they want to hear it again and again. Helping children begin to catch the rhythm of God's grace also helps parents, when times are tough, to remember God's faithfulness is new every morning (Lamentations 3:23) and salvation's story is wonderful year-round.

Being Helpful

Younger worshipers especially need help in learning how to pay attention in worship. Following are some ideas about listening to Scripture and participating in responsive readings and the shorter parts of some liturgies. Chapters to follow will deal fully with music, sermons, prayer and sacraments.

In the story of Jeremy, the little boy with a dog named Precious, I illustrated how exciting paying attention can be when a four-year-old participates in the responsive reading. I helped Jeremy, as I had helped my own boys, by allowing him to stand on the pew as I stood. This brought him up high enough that I could easily put my arm around him and hold the hymnbook that contained the reading in front of him. For toddlers, this stance also adds a measure of what I call "affectionate control." You are holding your child very close, but in a way that's more of a hug than a tug.

Then, as most toddlers know their colors, I was able to point to the words as we went along. In our responsive reading tradition, the pastor reads the black or plain print and the congregation the red or bold print. I told Jeremy to watch my finger as it pointed to "the black words that 'Uncle' Breck would read" and to listen carefully. I told him to watch my finger point to the red words and listen again. This method helps children to pay attention through sight as well as through hearing. It is worth mentioning here that congregations that use projected slides for singing and reading should print the words for children to have to help them participate. The point is to draw children to pay attention by helping them focus on what is happening and listen carefully to what is being said.

As soon as children are able to read even a few words, ask them to read the words they recognize and to listen to the meaning. As soon as children can read well, they can hold their own books and probably stand on the floor rather than on the pew. Older children should be able to identify the Scripture source for the responsive reading or the history of an alternative reading for a particular Sunday. For congregations using projected slides, older children are then trained to participate in the service, and the transition from print to distant projections doesn't distract them.

If children are trained to participate at a young age, their sense of belonging and paying attention is more natural. I am very saddened by the number of older children and teens I see just standing up looking bored through parts of the service

that they could participate in if they were asked and were
helped to do so.

During the reading of the Scripture, a bit of creativity can
help children to listen well. If the reading is a narrative or story,
young children can be asked to pretend that they were really
there when the action took place. Parents can draw attention to
the content of Scripture as it is read by asking questions: "How
do you think Jesus looked or sounded when he said this?" "How
would you feel if you had been there?" "What does the Scripture
say about how you felt yesterday?"

These questions are asked to get the child involved in every
part of worship. The child may respond with a whispered word or
phrase, or you may want to wait until you have left the sanctuary
before picking up the question again. As children are trained,
they get the idea of how and when to respond. Worship situations
and sanctuaries vary, but children who are responding to the
service are far less distracting to others than children who are
allowed to play in the pew.

With teens, questions about tone—"if this Scripture were a
movie scene"—or something pertinent to their lives can be
helpful. Let teens make comments to you as they make connec-
tions between Scripture readings and their lives.

Children will often get more out of Scripture readings than
you had expected. Sometimes they will hear a passage of
Scripture for the first time in a worship service, and they will
respond honestly. This can lead to some fascinating discussions about plagues, fire, how the Holy Spirit really operates
and many other topics. Kids have been known to want revenge
big-time when they hear about Herod, Judas Iscariot or other
biblical "bad guys."

Questions are good for children, and they are briefer than
explanations in a worship service that keeps moving along as

you parent in the pew. You usually will have time to ask only one question or make one comment to draw attention to each part of worship as it happens.

When we ask our children to pay attention, we often end up doing a better job of it ourselves. It is not unusual for parents to express delight as their own sense of worship is enhanced through practicing parenting in the pew. The liturgy becomes less routine and more relevant—not because the words have changed, but because we listen again to the familiar and find that God is still speaking.

Parenting in a Wiggly Pew:
The Challenge of Overactive Children

When I finish a "Parenting in the Pew" seminar at a church, I like to have a Q & A time. One question I nearly always get, whether in a group session or one on one privately, concerns the challenges of hyperactive children. "What can I do when my five-year-old won't sit still for more than ninety seconds?" Or "My son will sit fairly still, but his mind is in hyperdrive. He thinks all the time, notices everything and wants to talk, talk, talk." These parents frequently are exhausted, sigh pretty often and usually wish they hadn't attended the seminar. They wanted help in keeping their kids quiet, and there I was challenging them to keep their kids alert and engaged.

These parents love the Lord and their children. They want to do a good job but are overwhelmed with the personality of their bright, busy, squirmy and creative child. Whether or not their child has been officially diagnosed as hyperactive, they want help worshiping the Lord with him or her.

There is an ongoing debate over attention deficit disorder and attention deficit hyperactive disorder (ADD, ADHD), and I am not a professional therapist, counselor or researcher in this area. I do know that parents and church workers continue to deal with the realities of overactive and inattentive children in the life of the church. (Underactive and inattentive adults is a whole other book that I haven't written yet.)

The concerns of these parents are real. If a child is on a medication that is not to be given on weekends, then the Sunday morning challenge is an even bigger hurdle. But a few things may help make parenting in the pew possible even with the hyperactive child.

First, many of these children are *visual learners.* Writing things down helps them focus and learn. While my general recommendation is "no pencils, toys, coloring books, etc.," certain activities can help hyperactive visual learners pay appropriate attention and focus on worship. During certain parts of the service, toddlers and young schoolchildren could be allowed to draw pictures, and older schoolchildren and adolescents could take notes that reflect what the sermon or "long part" of the service is all about. The key is still to *concentrate on the service,* not just "do something." Parental control is the key here, just like all parenting in the pew. The parent can usually tell the difference between just doodling while distracted and drawing or writing in a way that extends the attention span.

One temptation is to put off including these children in the full service well past the age of four. There may be a few children who would benefit from this, but I've found the sooner overactive children are introduced to lengthy "sit still" times, the more helpful it can be. A few professionals have told me with anecdotal evidence that the principles I've outlined in this book are actually very good for ADD/ADHD children. It may take them longer to learn, and it may have to be relearned more often from week to week, but in the long run it may contribute to the health of these children.

Overactive children may have to be taken out of the sanctuary more often for disruptive behavior, but this is something parents must trust to the Lord and use as a means of training in humility. Parents of these often-gifted but easily distracted children need to take even more care than usual concerning where they sit in worship. What kinds of things and people most make your child hyper? Avoid them the best you can. I know that counselors who deal with ADD and ADHD students in the school setting recommend that these students sit near the front of the classroom.

In fact, sitting closer to "the action" is helpful for all children. It's a lot harder to help children participate in a service of worship if they sit toward the back of a sanctuary, too far to the side in a worship center or up in the "hidden" balcony. Parents sometimes choose these very spots for the times when kids act up, but I've discovered both in the classroom and in the sanctuary that kids actually are more attentive when sitting near the front.

During the Saturday preparation for worship, parents need to be intentional about pointing out appropriate expectations for children. Sometimes when children know what is expected (often linked to an age-appropriate reward at the end), they can cope better. A heightened sense of routine is often helpful. Most parents of ADD/ADHD kids know about dietary restrictions and allowances that are advisable and helpful, but this is beyond the scope of this book or my expertise.

Ask friends to help you when it's too hard or you're just too tired. Share with other parents and your pastor the challenges you feel in keeping up with your hyper children. Above all, pray for your children with thanksgiving. Ask the Lord to help you see your children through his eyes. Ask his help for patience, wisdom and strength to enjoy these kids. The creative giftedness that can make many Sunday mornings long can also make great saints in the long run.

Being Firm

Parenting in the pew goes better some weeks than others, for as many reasons as there are parents and kids. Being consistent is never easy. We all get tired. But I have been more consistent in worship training than in other parenting tasks. I think that's because it means more to me than other things, even food.

Being determined, however, does not preclude turmoil. As I began to share with parents what I had learned about parenting in the pew, I asked the boys, "What is the one thing I did that helped you more than anything to appreciate the importance of learning to worship?" They were about ten and eleven at the time. I asked each boy privately, out of the other's hearing. Much to my surprise, they gave an identical answer. I wasn't thrilled with their response, but I was the one who had asked. "Oh, Mama," each of them said, "it was the morning you marched me out and spanked my behind."

My only consolation was that each testified that this was a singular happening, but they knew I was serious from that time on. They went on to say that what followed the spanking—my earnest lecture on God's desire for their love and attentiveness—helped too.

I want to emphasize that there are big differences between kids, and differences in the way parents train their kids. Many parents refrain from corporal punishment and find other effective means to influence the behavior of their children. Sadly, some parents find it hard to control the extent of corporal punishment, and abuse results. Spanking can be counterproductive for some children. A privilege denied or another consequence may be just as motivating to some children. But empty threats and parental frustration aren't much help at all.

Whatever communicates to your child that you are serious about behavior in certain situations, whether it is the supermarket or the sanctuary, should be applied in private and with consistency. Being clear about expectations and consequence is very important, no matter how children are disciplined.

Robert and Scott received the discipline of spanking and were responsive to its intent. I am glad those days are over. My mom was right: it does hurt the parent more. I don't know why exactly Rob and Scott spoke of this as the most helpful part of their training. But I would be less than honest if I left this story out.

Proverbs 22 includes admonitions to parents to "start children off on the way they should go" (v. 6), to use corporal discipline wisely (v. 15), and to follow this advice with

Pay attention and turn your ear to the sayings of the wise;
    apply your heart to what I teach,
for it is pleasing when you keep them in your heart
    and have all of them ready on your lips.
So that your trust may be in the Lord,
    I teach you today, even you. (vv. 17-19, emphasis added)

Parenting in the pew is not easy, but I am grateful that my children learned, slowly but surely, that they can count on the God who encountered them in worship. It beats counting bricks.

6

make a joyful noise

the Atomic Praise Choir at our church was in full swing. Junior-high and high-school kids were enthusiastic about wearing tie-dyed T-shirts, tucked in, with blue jeans (no holes). They liked singing new hymns of the church, praise choruses and songs by artists heard on Christian radio.

Atomic Praise was a name cooked up in a brainstorming session with the kids in the choir. The idea was that this choir wanted to praise God with "every molecule" of their lives. Enthusiasm was high. As the choir director I could carry a tune, but I barely read music. I just wanted the church youth, Rob and Scott included, to discover what it might mean to worship the Lord with music. It was parenting in the pew on a massive scale.

The kids welcomed the challenge from the beginning. I let them know the rules up front. The girls couldn't believe I was serious about "no writing or passing notes." They all blinked when I told them they had to pay attention to the service. They sat up straight when I told them that we would have a test on the sermon every week at practice. (I'll tell you more about this in chapter eight.)

The thing that made it all worthwhile to them was the idea

that we were not going to perform for a congregational audience but praise God directly with our hearts and voices. Teenage molecules matter to the Lord. And music matters to teens. Putting the two together was a way to worship God with new insight and enthusiasm.

Music and Teenagers

Doctrine, theology and definitions of unfamiliar words are pretty far down on the list of teen interests. Good Christian music, new and old, gives an opportunity to teach the truth of Christian faith in a way that is more interesting to teenagers. The secular world certainly advertises its message through countless earphones plugged into adolescent audiophiles.

The Atomic Praise Choir discussed the message in the music. One Christmas we talked about what it meant for God to become "a man lost in time and space without rank or place." We talked about *atonement, redemption, hosanna* and *alleluia*. What do these words mean—not just in the dictionary, but in our hearts?

The most difficult thing for many teens is allowing the truths they learn in their heads to influence their real lives and behaviors. So many live compartmentalized lives. There is "church behavior" and then there is the-rest-of-the-world behavior. Within a downbeat after the last note of "Brother, Let Me Be Your Servant," the choir members' verbal putdown games would begin.

Sometimes with calm and patience and sometimes with an explosion of emotion, I would draw attention to this hypocrisy. Sometimes they listened. Sometimes they tuned me out. My efforts in practice to prepare them for worship were not in vain, but it was engaging in worship itself that meant the most. Connecting real gut appetites with understanding in the head is often a better way to get at the whole person.

Teenagers need to worship the Lord. When they are confronted by a reality beyond themselves, a reality that stands against the relativism of their culture, teens are comforted. The absolutes of the gospel revealed to us in Jesus Christ offer security and true freedom to teens living in a seductive world that tells them anything and everything just to make a sale. God's Word is not a sales pitch. It is the Truth. Worship gives teens a chance to meet the Truth-Teller up close and personal. Music is a good way to make the introduction.

However, introductions are best made one by one rather than on the mass scale I attempted with Atomic Praise. Through advocacy and interest, parents of teens can help their increasingly independent children worship through music. Listen to contemporary Christian music with your teens. Talk about words and meanings. Some of this music is fluff and meaningless repetition. But much of it contains new-wineskin insights of how the gospel relates to the world today.

Talk about the older hymns of the church. Define words and discuss meanings. Again, some of this music is fluff and meaningless repetition. But many hymns, the "oldies but goodies" that have lasted for centuries, distill the gospel into rhymes of truth. All hymns, whether written two years or two centuries ago, were new once.

J. S. Bach and Michael W. Smith, Stuart Townend and Martin Luther, the Gettys and the Wesleys have all expressed in music what the Holy Spirit has set in their hearts. Biblical truths set to music can be used by God to lead us to the throne of grace in worship. Talk to your pastor, worship leader, music director or worship committee about including a variety of sounds in sacred music.

Ethnic variety as well as style and generational variety help us express before the Lord what the kingdom of God is all about. The kingdom is young and old, from every tribe and nation. Teenagers, with their appetite for change and newness, can help an entire congregation better reflect the biblical kingdom that transcends cultures, generations and personal preferences.

Starting Young Helps

Teenagers were all toddlers once upon a time. Parents of toddlers think the high-school years will never come, while parents of teens think toddlerdom was just the day before yesterday. In all the seasons of childhood, there is music.

Jesus loves me, this I know;
For the Bible tells me so.

This is a toddler standard. It was also the reply of twentieth-century theologian Karl Barth when asked to summarize the essence of his faith. Truth can be learned to a tune played with two fingers. Barth argued for the revelatory nature of biblical authority in an extremely sophisticated and learned manner. Toddlers boom it out in church basements every Sunday.

Music is one of the easier tools for parents to use in teaching their children to worship. Music is prescribed in Scripture as a means to worship (Psalm 33:3 and 100:2, and Colossians 3:16 are just a few examples). In the next chapter I will discuss how praise and prayer are often expressed through music. Scripture memorizing, too, is made easier if done through songs.

Sunday-school music, however, is seldom the music of the sanctuary. Parents need help in getting the youngest of worshipers to sing praise to God through music written for adults. This can be a significant way that young children are connected to the heritage and history of the church. Worship music can also lay a foundation for understanding the truth of God that produces the theologians of the next century.

Training children to sing hymns and songs in the sanctuary is one of the easiest aspects of parenting in the pew. Children love being set free to "make a joyful noise." This opportunity is not to be missed! If a congregation uses overhead slides for words said or sung in worship, they should be printed out for children ten years and younger. Children find it harder to focus on text from a distance and will find it easier to participate, as they learn to read, to hold the text in their hands.

During songs or hymns, encourage very young children to sing "la, la, la" with the tune if the words are totally unknown or unpronounceable to them. Children don't mind doing this and will quickly begin to pick up the refrain or a repeated phrase.

Children can learn hymns more easily if the same hymn or song is sung several weeks in a row. A "hymn of the month" can be a great help to parents in the pew, especially those with pre-schoolers who as yet lack reading skills. If you think this would be helpful, ask your pastor, music director or worship committee to consider this as a ministry for the training of children. Even adults without children in the pew may not mind the repetition if it is seen as purposeful.

It is especially helpful for teens to know the history behind the writing of a hymn. Many classical as well as contemporary hymns have a story behind them that can enhance any worshiper's sense of reverence and joy, but especially teenagers who often question the relevance of traditions. The pastor or worship leader can tell these stories to the congregation. Also, many church libraries have books that tell the stories behind the hymns and their authors.

It is important to help children feel physically involved in worship. Even before they can read, they need to be able to hold a hymnbook or see the overhead screen. This usually means that toddlers and early grade-schoolers stand on the pew or chair next to their parent. The parent stands with one arm around the child, either holding the hymnbook or, if worship lyrics are projected, helping draw attention to the screen if printed material for children is not provided.

The parent should try to sing in such a way that the child can hear the song clearly, and when necessary the parent can give instructions. As a "single" parent between two children, I used one hymnbook for the three of us. One of the boys held the book while I pointed out the words with one finger, stanza by stanza. My other arm usually found itself around the child who wiggled the most that Sunday.

After they could read fairly well, each of the boys held a hymnbook, and I would sing out of one or the other. If your church uses an overhead screen, the same close-standing and directive methods can be used, but remember that it is harder for children to concentrate visually. They can be instructed and encouraged to listen even more attentively to the words. It's important to note that grade-school children developmentally find it harder to concentrate and focus well for a length of time on a distant screen, so it's good to have song lyrics, prayers, readings or anything used for congregational participation printed for children to use during the service. Many congregations that use overhead projection in worship print a children's bulletin just for this purpose.

Very young children can be asked to listen for a particular word or phrase in a song. They will join in with gusto as they catch on. One of my fondest memories of worship with my toddlers came during the singing of "Ask Ye What Great Thing I Know." After three or four lines, the declarative refrain is "Jesus Christ, the Crucified!" What a time my boys had waiting and listening for this line. At first I had to give them a cue—a nod of my head or a loudly whispered "Now!"—and they would sing out with toddler enthusiasm the joyous refrain.

As children get older, it's good to explain and discuss the content of hymns. This can be done prior to worship as you are settling in the pew. It can also be done at home with familiar hymns during informal times. Brief insights or meaning can be highlighted during the instrumental introduction to the song or hymn. Good worship leaders often help the congregation focus on the content or worship intention of church music, and parents can direct children to listen to and understand these explanations.

Always the integrity of heart and voice, of believing what is being sung, is important in worship. Some songs contain declarations that we would like to be true of us, but may highlight hypocrisy or shortcomings in our lives instead. We need to be able to talk about our struggle to "surrender all" to Jesus. We need to help our children understand that grace really *is* amazing—that once being lost and now being found, being blind and now seeing, are not just words to a song, but the testimony of what it means to be known by Jesus.

This can often be accomplished through simple, whispered expressions that help a child or teen know what you are thinking after a hymn is sung. I've often done this as we sat back in the pew after singing. "Jesus was sure my friend this week when I was worried about Grandpa" can enhance the meaningfulness of "What a Friend We Have in Jesus." Such remarks help children get the idea that what is sung really matters; it really counts in everyday life as well as Sunday worship. They learn to listen to the words they sing. They learn to live the words too.

Listening to Others' Music

Worship services often contain offerings of music that are not intended for the congregation's direct participation. Choral offertories and anthems are sung to God, while the congregation is invited to worship in a meditative way as the music leads. Young children can be taught to listen for a special word within a choral selection. They can squeeze your hand every time they hear the word *Jesus* or *glory*, for instance. In this way they learn to listen, pay attention and appreciate the words as well as the music. This is a helpful skill for older children who may not prefer the style of the music but can listen for truth in the lyrics.

Some music—instrumental preludes, offertories and postludes—is offered to the Lord without words. Children can be asked to listen closely and picture what is going on in the music. Parents can ask the child to think of a Bible story that seems to go along with the music. Not surprisingly, children find this quite easy to do. It may not be what the composer had in mind or match the piece's title in any way, but children "see" action in their imaginations suggested by the music. In worship, children can be reminded to think about God, creation, a Bible story or other sacred things as they listen. Is the music happy? sad? peaceful? turbulent? Children reared in the age of video have no problems thinking in pictures to music. Classical music is the background of choice for many cartoons.

To help children concentrate on sacred music, especially older music, in worship, it is wise to practice with wordless classical music. A great place to do this with less boredom and distraction is in the car. I began to train Rob and Scott in listening to all sorts of instrumental music when driving. I'd tune in a classical station or play an instrumental album track. Then I'd ask them to listen and think what kind of story or movie scene could happen to this music. In the sanctuary, where worship is the point, I usually suggested a general idea or theme, but in the car I did not. They would come up with anything—and they did! Great fugues were the backgrounds for shark attacks and car races. Quieter pieces were ladybugs in the grass or sneaky spies creeping up on someone. It was fun. And it helped.

In church the prelude might begin to remind them of Jesus when he fed the multitude. A lively offertory might be God creating the dinosaurs. It may not be what Handel (or whoever) had in mind, but the boys were learning to listen. It was a start.

One Easter season, our church choir led the congregation in a special Holy Thursday service. Most of the music was offered to the Lord by the choir alone. At the close of worship, we were to file out in silence as the sanctuary was darkened. Scott just sat back in the pew and whispered for me to go ahead. "I just want to sit here for a few minutes and think about stuff," he said. I was so grateful that he had learned to listen to music in worship.

Children's Choir

Children's choirs can be of great help in including young people's gifts in worship. Encourage your children to participate as an offering to God, not to perform for the congregation. Verbally reinforce this both before and after the service. Compliments can focus less on how the child did than on how worship was enhanced or how God was blessed. "I really thought a lot about how God loves me while you sang your song to the Lord this morning. Thank you for helping me worship" is very different from "Oh, I was so proud of you this morning. You sang so well." Children will hear the difference, and they will be reminded of what is important in worship. They will learn the vast difference between school programs and leading others in worshiping the living God.

The temptation to take pictures or video-record children's choirs in worship should be resisted. And congregations that use clapping as an expression of gratitude to God should be careful to teach children the difference between applause focused on a performance and the clapping of hands offered as praise to God.

Ain't No Rock!

There is a song I like to sing to the Lord that comes from Jesus' warning that if people do not praise him, the rocks will. This song also reflects on the psalms that declare that all creation gives praise to the Lord. Birds sing; trees wave their branches. This song, with its very old sentiment, is put to a contemporary beat, sort of an old gospel spiritual sound. It is a joy to sing.

When teaching children how to worship, parents must remind them that their "chief end" is the glory of God. We need to make a joyful noise before the Lord in worship. We need to "sing to the Lord a new song." We need to show our children what it means to begin to enjoy the Lord forever through biblically faithful and lyrically rich contemporary music.

And our children need to enter into the heritage of faith left to us by songwriters in ages past.

> What language shall I borrow
> > to thank Thee, dearest friend,
> > for this Thy dying sorrow,
> > thy pity without end?
> O make me Thine forever;
> > and should I fainting be,
> > Lord, let me never, never
> > outlive my love to Thee.
> > > (Bernard of Clairvaux, 1091–1153)

7

prayer, confession and canned goods

my mother tells me that when I was very young, I had an invisible friend named Werff. She remembers that this creature was very small and very near, and that I was adamant about where Werff was, what he liked to eat and things I heard him say. Werff was occasionally stepped on, sat on or inadvertently interrupted, but my friend always recovered. Werff seems to have disappeared somewhere, though, when my sister Kellie was born.

Children have the capacity to speak to and listen to what is unseen. The faith they possess to do so is part of what Jesus commended as the very faith that gives evidence of the kingdom of God. Children can know what it is to pray in faith to an unseen God who is a real friend.

If our children learn to pray, to speak to God and to hear him speak to them, a solid foundation of faith can be set in their lives. And because God is real and well able to establish communication with our children, he will not fade away like imaginary childhood friends.

Praying, Not Parroting

Parents, pastors and Christian educators often do not give children enough opportunities to enter into the prayer life of church or home. Children may be taught to "say grace" and "God-bless-so-and-so," but little else. Children need to be trained to pray and not parrot Christian phrases. Saying grace and praying "God bless" are not necessarily parroting, but they can be if these prayers are taught the same way as lines to a kindergarten play or how to say "please" and "thank you."

Children can be taught to pray by entering at an early age into the uncertainties as well as the joys of prayer. I remember one night Robert was wheezing with asthma. As a seven-year-old, he struggled with the idea that Jesus *could* heal, but had not healed him. After many prayers of his own, along with ours and those of the elders of the church, Robert surprised me with a faith that I sometimes struggled to reach myself. Between heavy breaths, he prayed, "Jesus, I know that you know best. I sure would like to be better, but whatever you do is okay with me."

About a year later, Robert prayed the night before my husband had to have knee surgery, "Dear Jesus, please make Daddy's knee all better so when the doctors see it tomorrow they will be surprised that they don't have to fix it. Well, I know you always do what's best, so if you decide not to do what I really want, well, that's . . . " He paused and then haltingly yet deliberately continued, "okay . . . because . . . you . . . are still . . . well . . . Jesus."

Scripture is full of wonderful stories of heart's-desire prayers answered. It is also full of honest disappointment in prayer. Children can handle both. If prayer is to become real to children, if God is to become real to them, faith must find its foundation in real-life experiences with God in prayer. God must be trusted to say yes or no as he determines how best to love us.

Home Training for Corporate Prayer

Structures for different types of prayer can be found in the corporate worship of the church. Most liturgies contain times for confession, intercession and praise. These times of congregational prayer are an important part of training children to trust God with their lives and to know the needs and support of God's greater family.

A crucial element of preparing children for congregational prayer is prayer in the home. From the earliest age, children should be encouraged to speak to God in their own words. You can probably teach them best by sharing prayers in your own words with them. Children need to hear their parents "just talk" to God. They need to see us, and to sit with us eventually, as we listen to God in silence.

Prayer needs to be woven into the fabric of our lives. Children need to see that prayer is central to our faith-filled dependence on God. They need to see that prayer is not frivolous wishing-with-amen-at-the-end. I don't pray for parking spots just because I'm running late. But my children have heard me pray for a parking spot on a busy street in front of the doctor's office when Scott had a 105-degree temperature and it was pouring rain. And they've been able to *marvel* in the New Testament sense when we parked in that spot.

Honesty in Prayer

Scott prayed one night when he was four, "Jesus, thank you for all the beautiful things in the world, and all the canned goods." This is how I found out about the collection for canned goods in the Sunday school. Scott was also famous for being grateful for chicken as a toddler. It was his favorite food. Still is.

Children need to talk to God about the things that concern their lives. As parents, we need to be honest about situations in our world and our lives that we do not understand. Children have a sense about what is real or not real to us.

Most children get suspicious at an early age about the actual existence of Santa Claus and the tooth fairy. God needs to be in a different category. In fact, though a full discussion of this topic goes beyond the scope of this book, I will admit that we never did practice traditions of fantasy-as-fact in our home. It was fine to pretend, to nurture imagination, but we decided not to present that which is not real as real. It helped cut down on a whole lot of disappointment and confusion. Santa Claus was treated like Donald Duck or Mickey Mouse, a fun person in costume with a made-up story. (We did tell the boys it was fine to pretend with friends and that many of their friends might not know what was up and that was okay.) Actually, we decided not to keep most of the traditions of our culture that have come to be associated with the holidays of the church. Whether or not other parents do as we did, it is important for our kids to sense a clear difference between Jesus and the Easter Bunny.

God is believable because he is real. His reality rings true with children because of his sovereignty. God's purposes and will do not always match our expectations. It is very often in disappointment or difficulty in the lives of our children that God's existence becomes objective and real, distinctive and powerful for them. We shouldn't be afraid that prayer that is not answered according to our hopes will weaken or destroy our children's faith. Children need to see that God can be trusted no matter what. This is the foundation for maturing faith.

Once a college student lived a short while with a family in our church. She needed some shelter and encouragement after a particularly difficult emotional crisis. The family she stayed with does a very good job of prayer and Scripture training in their home (and worship training in the pew). While staying with this family, the student lost her job. After family prayers for her predicament, the six-year-old sought out the weeping, fearful student. This little child of faith put her arm around her sad "big sister" and told her matter-of-factly, "You know God knew about this day even before you were born. So if he knows all about it and it's okay with him, well, it will be okay."

The student was able to share with me and with the couple she was staying with that Psalm 139 was never more real to her than in the confident understanding of this very young child. Such is the kingdom. Learning to pray about real things, simple or profound, prepares children to participate in the church family.

The church needs to hear the prayers of children, because they often reflect the best definition of faith given in the Scripture: "Faith is confidence in what we hope for and assurance about what we do not see" (Hebrews 11:1).

Prayer for Grubby Hearts

Forgiveness is one of our most hoped-for yet unseen needs in life. It is realized through faith that finds expression in prayers of confession. In worship services, prayers of confession are usually followed by the pastor's or worship leader's declaration of forgiveness based on the finished work of Jesus, using a promise of Scripture. This can be an important experience for a child.

During prayers that include a time for personal, silent confession, very young children should probably be guided by quiet whispers. It goes something like this: "Now is the time we bow our heads and talk to Jesus about stuff we are sorry about. Remember our talk this morning about being selfish? Tell Jesus about this now, and ask him to help you share the last doughnut with your brother (or mother!) next time."

One confession dear to my heart (and I'm sure to God's) went something like this, "Dear Jesus, you cleaned up my heart last week and now it is all grubby again. I need some help!" I bet the sermon that week was from Romans 7. I do know that this young grade-schooler was learning to talk honestly with the Lord.

A toddler can be encouraged to confess any recent no-no, but it should be something that he or she actually remembers, something that is not more than a day old. Fortunately for purposes of training in confession, this is not a problem for the normal toddler. But should children come to worship with a "clean slate," confession time can be used as a time to "thank Jesus for loving us no matter what."

Prayer for Patience

As we parent our children to love God, we need to guard against charging every situation with a deeply spiritual lesson. "Don't judge October apples in June" was probably the best advice I ever received as a young mother concerned with the willfulness of one of my toddlers. It is a mark of our own maturing faith in God *not* to try to play Holy Spirit in the lives of our children.

True repentance, genuine spiritual insight and real faith are the fruits of the Holy Spirit's work in our lives and the lives of our children. The apostle Paul reminds us, "For we are God's handiwork, created in Christ Jesus to do good works, which God prepared in advance for us to do" (Ephesians 2:10).

The longing in our hearts for our kids to "turn out right" can cause us to make a mountain out of every molehill in our child's life. Every scratch, sneeze, milk spill or childish sin is not an occasion for a sermon or spiritual lesson. Sometimes it's hard to relax with our own kids. It can be difficult to see the humor in their antics, even though we laugh about the same things done by other people's kids.

Parenting can be stressful. Especially if we try to take on God's job as well as our own. It is God's job to be working in the lives of our children. His work is lasting, wise, patient and all-knowing. We parents, no matter how well we succeed at times, fall short in all four categories. He alone is the perfect Parent who loves our children perfectly. We must trust him to be at work in the lives of our children, even when this is hard to do.

As our children grow, they need to confess sin as they see it. Prayers need to become increasingly filled with the concerns they bring up. Parents need to trust the Lord with the spiritual growth of our children. I believe that God is writing a testimony in the lives of our children. It is his story. He alone sees the end from the beginning. He alone sees the October apples when it is only June.

Prayer in the Church

Prayer that is specific, concrete and arising from real-life situations fosters honesty with God that can lead to a lifetime of experiencing redemption and grace. This kind of praying by children can encourage the same kind of real honesty in the prayer life of our congregations. Corporate prayer in the church is all too often superficial and filled with parrot-like religious phrases.

"Dear God, don't let Tommy get killed in the war" was the prayer on all of our hearts but on none of our adult lips one Sunday—until a child prayed the prayer we all wanted to pray. Sunday-school teachers and trusted friends need to pray with the child who blurts out one morning, "My daddy has a girl-friend and doesn't love us anymore." The honest prayers of children remind us that our Father knows all the details, all the struggles, all the answers.

Many children are the masters of details that we soon forget—or wish we could. Training children in prayers of intercession can be an adventure in remembering. Young children who hear about someone in the church who is very ill will remember to pray for that person even when we don't. This is especially true if they are allowed to visit the sick person.

When visiting does not hinder the well-being of the ill person, children can often be the very best of visitors. Such visits are usually brief and followed by a million questions, especially if they take place in a hospital. Much information about expectations should be given before the visit, and patient explanations are needed afterward. Seeing the sick person, feeling a part of his or her experience, helps children from toddlers to teens to pray with more care, insight and genuine faith. And the sick person is usually glad for an honest visitor who wants to know "what that is" and doesn't just make small talk.

Prayer is a major part of being a church family. Our children need to be a part of our relationships within that family. The answers God gives us as a family of faith are his way of loving us and encouraging our trust.

It all starts with little things. Teaching very young children to fold their hands and close their eyes is a way to enhance their ability to concentrate on what they are doing. These gestures are not prayer in and of themselves, but a means to that end. They need to be taught, shown, retaught and explained in that context. I've noticed that parents are often more intentional (and more enthusiastic) in teaching children the gestures and words to a favorite team's fight song than they are in teaching children how to pray. Christian parents don't intend by this to communicate which is actually more important to them, but sometimes I think we are better at making new fans than we are at making new disciples.

Prayer for the World

Prayer must be more than ritual and gesture for our children and young people. Teaching children to pray for the mission concerns of the church can be enhanced by real-life visits from people from the country in which a church has a missionary or a mission concern. Very often an inquiry with the international student office at a local university can put the church in contact with students from all over the world. Lonely international students are more than eager to be invited to meet others and tell about their home and culture. Sometimes these students are not Christian, and your initiative in reaching out can spark friendships and opportunities to share the gospel.

International Christians should be given opportunities to pray with congregations in their native language. What a vivid reminder that God loves the whole world and listens to prayer in any language.

Children are influenced greatly by the international students who are invited into our homes and congregations. Children learn that the world is broader than their own hometown; their geography skills are improved; and they learn to eat just about anything. And they learn to pray for others around the world with a fondness and warmth that is radically different from the prejudice and isolationism found in many teens outside the church.

Prayers of Praise

Praise is one of the easier aspects of prayer for children to learn. Expressions of thanks come fairly easy for young people. If traditional hymns are used in liturgy, very often one will be a hymn of praise. Point this out to your children. Seeing prayer in the lyrics can be an important help as you teach your children to praise God.

Helping children identify a truth about God's character can help them learn to praise God for who he is. A hymn, a sermon illustration or a phrase in a creed can highlight a characteristic of God. This can be used to help children focus on a single aspect of God and to give thanks.

Current events in congregational life can also bring into focus how God's character affects our daily life. A family in our church once lost their home in a fire. In the worship service, thanksgiving was given for God's safekeeping. Mention was made of God's presence and power at work in waking a family member before any smoke entered the bedroom areas of the home. That morning we sang hymns that confessed God as sovereign, God as a hiding place and God as the giver of peace. This was good opportunity for parents in the congregation to help their children focus on the character of God and to give the Lord praise for making himself so evident in the lives of the people they knew.

Drawing children to a life of praise and gratitude is vital in a world so full of discontent and restlessness. One four-year-old in our congregation dissolved in quiet tears during a praise song one Sunday. The Scriptures tell us that the Holy Spirit helps us pray with "groans that words cannot express." Little Sarah was moved by the music and words of a sung prayer of praise. Her tears were the purest expression of prayer. Her mom held her quietly and shared that moment with her, reassuring her that it was a good way to feel toward God. Once this same little one had misbehaved and I had heard her whisper, "Oh, Mommy, don't take me out." To stay, to be a part, to be involved in the worship of God is important to Sarah. She is learning that her presence and her parents are important parts of that experience.

Teens in Prayer

Until high-school days, our family had devotions with prayer and Bible reading as a family each morning before we were off to school and work. We used devotional guides at times. The series from Youth for Christ is especially well written and doesn't talk down to kids. There are a variety of Bible study guides, some designed specifically for teens, which we used for an evening study. Have your teen ask your pastor, youth worker or parachurch minister what they might recommend.

As high-school days started, the boys began to have a "devo" in the morning on their own, with Bible readings they chose themselves. Some days were better than others. They had to be reminded. The boys began to learn how different a day could be based on whether or not they had spent time with the Lord. After personal "devo" time, we would have family prayer together. This practice was enhanced by a summer experience in the wilderness on a mission trip. The spiritual richness of an extended time each morning in prayer and Scripture was one of the main reasons the boys signed up for a second summer.

Teenagers in a charismatic community can begin to embrace expressions of faith that are evident in their parents and congregations, like speaking in tongues and the laying on of hands. With all types of churches and kids, there are seasons of spirituality that must be encountered and entrusted to God. Raising hands and using tongues in praise are important to parents in some charismatic and Pentecostal communities. Parents who worship in this tradition naturally want their children to share in these expressions.

Smaller children will often cheerfully imitate what they see, and parents then simply need to teach them the meaning and practice of these traditions. Many parents become concerned, however, when junior-high and older young people back off and become more guarded in their outward participation.

For kids of all congregational stripes, the teen years are a typical time to step back and evaluate why they are doing what they are doing. This can be a wonderful time for parents to share histories and stories of faith. But we also need to share stories of failure. Sometimes the latter will be more encouraging to a young person who is struggling with doubts and questions. This can be the stuff of grown-up prayer. David's psalms of paradoxical doubt and faith can help teens stay close to the Lord in times of struggle. (See Psalms 10, 13, 40 and 142 for examples.)

Teens need to begin to own their faith. Their expressions of faith need to come increasingly from their hearts and less from help parents have provided. The gifts of the Spirit are truly *gifts*. This is the time when they need to open up their lives and hearts in the way the Spirit directs. Parents will not always see what we want to see in our children's lives, but then God's ways are not our ways.

Let hands be raised, expressions of gifts come forth and works of service be offered as the Lord directs. Our children need to be with us in the pew. Hearing God's Word can touch their hearts and teach them in ways we cannot see.

We need to pray for our teens. A lot. And they need to know about our struggles of faith. This will do more to help them share their struggles with us and with the Lord than almost anything else.

Teens also need to be encouraged to take risks, costly risks, for the Lord. Short-term summer missions to places of challenge and deprivation can be the very best training experiences in prayer. Prayer is what it should be when there are no options. Out of teens' own experiences with God in the pew or in Peru, God can fashion young men and women who love him with all their hearts.

Prayers of Silence

Learning to listen in prayer is hard for all of us in our very noisy society. Our silence, however, gives God a chance to get a word in edgewise. Training in silence can be introduced in the later teen years, but even as they are growing up, children need to know that silence is an important part of their parents' prayer life. And if listening in prayer is a "growing edge" for you, maybe you can grow with your teen in this regard.

When Rob and Scott were fifteen and sixteen, I began to teach them about letting Scripture enhance the practice of silence in prayer. I took advantage of an opportunity when they had seen a group of college students practice this form of prayer, so they were very receptive. (Parents need to expose teens to alternative mentors in the faith. It is good to listen to teens and pick up on which people of faith communicate well with them. College students were big for my kids.)

For our first "retreat of silence," the two boys and I sat in a quiet room together and asked the Lord to bring to each of our minds a story about Jesus from Scripture. It could be any story, I reassured them. When one came to mind, I told them just to sit there and try to visualize the place, sounds, scene, people and Jesus. As they lingered in the scene, I asked each of them to pray silently and invite the Lord to teach them something as they revisited this biblical event.

For our first attempt at silence in prayer, I limited the time to twelve minutes. As they listened for God's voice, I silently asked the Lord to speak a word of grace and truth to my sons. I was shocked (O ye of little faith!) to find out that God took just those twelve minutes to put his finger on some of the deepest issues of faith and obedience in their lives. I had never heard Rob and Scott reflect more clearly on what God was seeking to do in their lives. That first experience of God's "talking back" in prayer helped them begin to discern his voice as distinct from their own. I continued fairly regular sessions of silent prayer with my boys from junior high through high school. It was often helpful to choose and read a particular Scripture and then just help them use their five senses to enter imaginatively into the biblical scene.

Many young people ask, "How do you hear God speak to you? How do you tell that it is God?" The answer is necessarily ineffable. It is something you *know* deeply and distinctly. Using Scripture to guide this kind of listening in prayer is helpful. It is especially important for young Christians and for teens who tend to be emotional in how they perceive God's direction and nearly everything else.

The thing that struck me after that first attempt at silent meditation in prayer was how *easy* it was for Rob and Scott. I realized that the boys were able to concentrate quite easily on the Scripture-scene because they had been trained from their early years to listen intently and vividly to the reading of Scripture and its exposition in sermons.

Parenting in the pew has helped my children in more ways than I ever could imagine. In September, I began to see my October apples mature.

8

just how long was that sermon?

Eutychus is definitely the patron saint of everyone who has fallen asleep during a sermon. His story is recorded in the book of Acts:

> Seated in a window was a young man named Eutychus, who was sinking into a deep sleep as Paul talked on and on. When he was sound asleep, he fell to the ground from the third story and was picked up dead. Paul went down, threw himself on the young man and put his arms around him. "Don't be alarmed," he said. "He's alive!" . . . The people took the young man home alive and were greatly comforted. (Acts 20:9-10, 12)

There is more than a little instruction for parents in this story. The first is that Eutychus should never have been sitting on the window sill. He should have been with his parents in the pew. He might have still fallen asleep (Paul's sermon started at sundown on Sunday and didn't end until midnight), but it would have caused less commotion. Actually, probably more than a few people present secretly welcomed the unfortunate distraction. As it was, Paul just put his arms around the boy, pronounced him alive and then picked up his sermon where he loft off, preaching on "until daylight" (v. 11).

This story is a valuable one to keep in mind the next time your kids complain about sermons being too long. Let them know it could be longer, even lethal. But of greater help to parents is Paul's encouragement, "Don't be alarmed. He's alive!"

The "don't be alarmed" part, of course, came easily for Paul, a single man who had no children. Nevertheless, we parents are still to take heart. There is not a saint alive that has managed to stay awake during every sermon she or he ever heard.

The different personalities and attention spans of children make a wide variety of behaviors possible when the "long part" of the worship service begins. Concentrating on the sermon is one of the hardest parts of worship for children of all ages—even when Daddy is the preacher. Helping children listen to and learn from the sermon takes persistence, creativity and time. It also helps to have a pastor who thinks of children as well as adults during sermon preparation.

Learning to listen to God's Word as it is read, taught and proclaimed is an important part of how children begin to discern the unique authority of Scripture for the church. I once had the opportunity to spend week-long quality time with a beloved six-year-old girl, my granddaughter, Tyler. We were visiting family and friends and decided to go to worship with two different congregations on Sunday as a part of our visit. The first service we went to was rather traditional, and the second was a very contemporary "seeker service."

I was curious what this child thought about these two different congregational styles and how she perceived "worship." So, without a hint of my own opinion, I asked her which service she thought Jesus might have liked the best. She thought about it for some time—two minutes is quite a long time for a six-year-old to think. Finally she said, "Well, I liked them both, but I think Jesus really liked the first one better." Surprised, I asked her why. And her reply was, "Well, I think Jesus really likes the Bible, and there was more Bible in the first one."

Now, let me be clear, this six-year-old wasn't making a comment about style, but she was commenting on substance. Frankly, I was more than a bit surprised by her comment, but I found her reasoning insightful. Jesus does like Scripture. So take the advice of a six-year-old: no matter the style of congregational worship, make sure there is plenty of God's Word to anchor all that is said and done and sung.

Tuning in Young Children

Very young children need their attention drawn to the parts of a sermon that are illustrative. "Listen to this story" is a way of directing attention to parts of the sermon that can be most easily understood by youngsters.

Jesus told parables because a picture really is worth a thousand words; for most of us, stories are easier to grasp than abstractions. Pastors often use illustrations to help make a point they want their flock to take home. All people—but especially children—remember stories. As a part of the children's sermon or just before the "long" sermon, it's a great idea to have the pastor who will preach that service ask the children to listen for one particular word or short phrase that will be said several times. Ask a young child to squeeze your hand every time he or she hears that word or phrase to help him or her learn to listen. Ask an older child to note how the word or phrase is used or in what context or story throughout the sermon. Some pastors ask the children to count how many times the word or phrase is used and to tell them when they shake hands before leaving the sanctuary after the service.

Both children and pastors enjoy this.

Short sermons just for children are often included as a part of worship. Often grade-school and younger children are asked to come forward to sit near the front for a special message. Pastors may use this time to share the truth of Scripture with the youngest parishioners.

The children's sermon works best if it relates directly to the "adult sermon" that usually comes later in the worship service. This is a good opportunity for the pastor to tell a story or give an illustration that relates to children's lives and also to a major point of the day's sermon. Children's sermons need to deal with real issues and questions of faith in the lives of young people. It is best if children are taught something of substance in an illustrative way, but the point should not be lost in creative entertainment that only detracts from what is important.

In his book *Peculiar Speech: Preaching to the Baptized*, William Willimon comments on how much ministry for children is easily trivialized and fails to meet youngsters' spiritual needs. He writes, "The Bible has the courage to discuss such concerns. Why can't we speak to children with as much depth and complexity as the Bible uses? With what sort of honesty would we have to speak of our family life if we spoke with the words of the Bible rather than with the language of sentimentality and trivialization?" (Grand Rapids: Eerdmans, 1992, p. 55).

The responsibility of the children's sermon may be delegated to a youth worker, church leader or parent in the congregation, but I believe the pastor is the best person to give it. This helps children identify the pastor as a special teacher, a person to pay attention to and listen to. Admittedly, not all pastors are particularly gifted in interacting with or talking to children. In that case other spiritual leaders and people gifted in children's ministry should be encouraged to give the children's sermon.

The pastor can provide oversight and information about the substance of the adult sermon and can lend support to the person who teaches the children.

Guidelines and Ideas for the Children's Sermon

It's not unusual for congregations who welcome children in the sanctuary for "big people's church" to shy away from having a moment in the service especially focused on children. Disasters from the inclusion of children's sermons are legion. Pastors and worship leaders clearly remember telling the person handling this time that it must be short and simple—and the next thing you know it's a puppet show that "somehow" took twenty minutes, and no one knew how to stop it. Or how about the time the well-meaning but theologically inarticulate children's worker unknowingly taught the children the exact opposite point of the pastor's sermon? To avoid some of these disasters and to encourage the appropriate inclusion of an experience focused on young disciples, I offer the following guidelines.

First, to some extent, children gauge their importance by who pays attention to them—as we all do. Kids know who's in charge at church. So, given leeway for at least some giftedness with children, it's best if the person preaching the "long" sermon also gives the children's sermon. The preaching pastor knows what will become the main point and can think through a simple and illustrative way to share this with children.

Second, keep this time well-focused and brief. The whole process, including "travel time," should not take more than four to five minutes in most sanctuaries or worship centers. When children do come forward, they should still face the same direction as the congregation. Sitting children on steps facing the congregation gives them the sense that they are on display or expected to perform in one way or another. Also, it's hard to resist waving at your children or grandchildren while they are "up there."

In addition, if the children face the congregation, the pastor's back is to the congregation, and this is less than ideal for also communicating with and including the adults in the congregation in the children's moment from time to time. Most importantly, children need to have the sense that they are participating in this moment as members of the congregation—they belong there *with* God's gathered people.

Third, the experience should make one well-illustrated point and one only. The point of children's time isn't to give a short version of the whole sermon to come, but to help children catch the main point of God's Word that is central to that service of worship. So, visual aids should be able to be held in one hand and should big enough to be easily seen by the gathered children. The most important thing is that any visual or other aide used should be simple and its use should not distract from the main point.

The preaching pastor should think about the children's sermon main point and how to illustrate it while studying for and preparing, writing and practicing the exposition of God's Word. Simplicity takes more thought, not less. It takes time to get good at this too. Seminary students are seldom taught how to connect with children like this, so it's tempting to just eliminate this time or let other people try one from time to time. The former is regrettable, but the latter is the formula for disasters like the ones mentioned in the beginning of this section.

Here are a few simple ideas that have worked well for a child-focused moment in congregational worship. (These simple ideas may also give parents an idea of how to help children learn spiritually day-to-day.)

If the main point of the long sermon centers on the image of

God and how this makes people valuable and loved by God, all
the pastor needs is a twenty-dollar bill. The pastor holds up the
bill and asks the kids what "this" is—trust me, two-year olds
know. Then the pastor can ask, "Who would like this money?"
Every hand goes up (the dream of many evangelistic pastors
during the invitation). Then the pastor crumples up the bill,
stomps on the bill, even tears a little corner off the bill while the
children watch. Then the pastor says, "Oh, wow, this twenty-
dollar bill is a big mess. Would any of you still want this?"
Again, every hand goes up, and every child cries out, "Yes!"

Then the pastor says, "You know sometimes we're like a
twenty-dollar bill, all crumpled up and messed up and not too
good looking. But God still says he wants us, we're valuable to
him no matter what. Why? Because, just like this bill, there is
something stamped on us that tells us we're valuable. See this 2
and this 0?—and there are words printed on this bill that say
'legal tender' from the government. That means, crunched up
and messed up or not, this money is still worth what it was
when it was brand-new. God has printed something in you and
me, and in your moms and dads and grandparents too. It's his
own image—inside of us is an imprint of God himself. And, no
matter what, we are valuable to God. I want you to remember
this, okay?"

Then the pastor might close with a prayer or a reminder to
listen for the word *image* or another word or phrase when the
long sermon explains this idea more.

If a pastor (or parent at home) wants to teach about the importance of worship to children, here is a delightful way to go
about it. The pastor brings out two gift bags and tells the
children they are going to a birthday party, and they don't know
what present to bring. One gift bag is colorful and gorgeous
with ribbons and bright paper sticking out the top. The other

gift bag is a paper bag with a rip in the side and newspaper sticking out the top. The pastor holds them both up and says, "Which one do you think I should take to my friend's party?" (Note: don't complicate the point by naming the friend, just in case a child has a friend with that name—they can go nuts with joy on the spot.) All the kids point to the colorful gift bag and yell out, "That one! That one!" Then the pastor explains that they are certainly right, because it is obvious that lots of care went into this gift and how it is wrapped.

The pastor then takes a few moments to talk about how worship is our gift to God, and it matters to God that we wrap it carefully and thoughtfully. That's why this looks this way or this is done that way, the pastor says, while drawing attention to particular things in the immediate worship space. Then the pastor closes with prayer or the special "word of the day" for the sermon to come, all with the challenge for children to make their participation in worship a wonderful gift to God.

Simple. Focused. Use an idea that connects with children's lives. Not only do children, at least from time to time, get the point, but pastors tell me the adults listen to the long sermon a bit more attentively too.

The children's sermon is also a good opportunity for children to pray out loud and in unison. Such a prayer is led by the adult and echoed by the children, and its content should relate to the children's sermon. This helps children learn how to pray out loud within the congregation. It also teaches them that prayer is a good way to respond to Scripture when it is heard and understood.

Adults, in hearing the children's sermon, are helped by anticipating the focus of the sermon, possibly being introduced to the Scripture text and gaining a picture of what the exposition of the biblical text may contain.

Learning to Listen Little by Little

Help children listen to adult sermons by encouraging them to listen when stories are being told. If your pastor rarely or never uses story illustrations, share this idea for helping you as a parent in the pew. Preachers want people to listen to what they have prepared, and most will be encouraged by your interest. There are books, whole volumes in fact, and lots of online helps for pastors that contain sermon illustrations.

When the boys were quite young, I never worried much if they fell asleep during the sermon. After all, in most schools, kindergartners still take naps. And attention spans vary among children. But I wanted the boys to know that sermons are an important way to learn and to be challenged by the Word of God. Reviewing the highlights after the service was one way I let them know the sermon was important.

I asked questions. "That was a good story today in the sermon. What did you learn about God in the story about the lighthouse?" As children get older, you can ask questions that will push them to listen for details. "That was a neat story about how the famous Mr. Moody came to believe in Jesus. What did the man who shared the gospel with Mr. Moody do for a living?" General questions can work with older youth who have become good listeners. "So, what did you learn from the sermon today?"

Turnabout is fair play. Kids will ask their parents questions, too, as they begin to really listen to sermons ("Dad, what's a eunuch?"). Some kids will ask about the meanings of words. There will be phrases or expressions or intimations within a sermon that children will not grasp. Most of the time children just let things beyond their understanding slip past them. Sometimes they whisper questions in the pew. Giving brief answers to some questions is appropriate; others need to be answered later. Either way, be sure to respond respectfully to your children. If a question needs to be answered later, ask the child to remember the question and ask it again after church. If the question is truly important or interesting, the child will not forget to ask. And she or he will actually listen to the information or answer you give.

Some questions are answered as the sermon progresses. When you become aware that the child's question is being addressed from the pulpit, draw the child's attention to it. A quick whisper, with a nod of the head or a poke in the side, can tune a child in to the sermon just as his or her question is being answered. A great benefit to letting the sermon itself address questions is the way attention spans are lengthened. Children get the idea that to *keep listening* can be helpful.

Of course, not all sermons are put together or preached in a way that helps parents who are encouraging their children to pay attention. Again, making the most of the sermon after the service is often the only way. One parent shared with me that she let her kids draw a picture of what they heard in the sermon as it was being preached. It sounded like a good idea, but you need to discern when or if this becomes doodling and game playing. If this becomes a problem, I would suggest that the children draw pictures of what they learned *after* the service and that the family discuss the sermon together.

Once I was talking about parenting in the pew with the father of a nine-year-old. He told me that he let his grade-schooler bring a "Find Waldo" book to church for the sermon time. He had simply never thought about asking his son to listen. He liked the idea of beginning with stories and illustrations. I encouraged my friend to leave Waldo at home and to work at helping his son find the joy of worship instead.

Some churches provide pads with puzzles, games and space to draw to keep children occupied during the long parts of worship. Not only is the use of these pads not confined to the long parts, but it supports the idea that it is okay for kids to tune out during worship. The pads are provided to keep kids quiet, not to train them in worship. Using them may be easier, but the reward is paltry. "Worship aides" for children are often well-intended but unhelpful invitations to not pay attention in worship. Unfortunately, this habit (with higher-priced distractions) can linger well into adulthood.

Speaking of adulthood, how about the challenge for children *and* adults not to play with electronic gadgets during worship? If your Bible is on your iPhone, Kindle, iPad or whatever, the temptation to be distracted after the Scripture reading can be pretty high. So, along with your children, shut off everything during the worship that doesn't help you or your children focus on what is really happening in real time and in a real place.

Older Children and Sermons

After a "Parenting in the Pew" seminar, one teenager in our congregation "had" to sit with his parents again. This high-school sophomore joined his family as they all started over together in learning to worship. After a few weeks, I asked Chad whether he was still speaking to me and how he was doing.

He smiled easily and responded, "Oh, I like it. I never knew I could understand a sermon before. I don't mind at all."

I wish I had lots of stories like Chad's to tell you. Usually I don't get to visit a church other than the time I have worship consultations for congregations using *Parenting in the Pew*, so most stories like Chad's are unknown to me. I did get a note once that related how the father of a seven-year-old noticed how unusually attentive his son was during the sermon time one Sunday. This dad sang in the choir and could see his family in the pew easily. This young boy's mom had attended a seminar

I had for the congregation the previous Saturday. When asked about his attentiveness, the son matter-of-factly told his dad that it was "the best sermon I ever heard." The second-grader went on to explain that he was able to pay attention "because Mom wouldn't let me do anything else."

I have found that young people like to be challenged. Parents need to expect more from their children in church. Sophomore Chad and this seven-year-old were asked to pay attention to a sermon; when they did, they discovered the long part was meant for them too.

The Atomic Praise Youth Choir made the same discovery. The choir had made significant progress in entering into the worship of God on Sundays. These junior-high and high-school kids were getting it. They paid attention and participated in readings, hymns, prayer and Scripture, and their music was increasingly directed toward God and not the congregation.

But when it came to sermon time, a sudden transformation took place. Alertness became lethargy, bright eyes became dull, and "teen slump" became the posture of choice. All this happened in the time it took for the Scripture reading to end and the pastor to pronounce the first word of his sermon. Why?

It was the lack of expectation. The kids had been tuning out habitually since childhood and had never been expected to listen. I couldn't poke all of them in the ribs, so I had to be creative. But not really all that creative; it didn't take much.

At choir practice, I shared my concern about the importance of listening to the sermon, the teaching of Scripture. After the "why," I suggested a training incentive. Every week at practice, I would ask three questions drawn from the sermon. I might ask about a detail in a story the pastor told, the reference from which the sermon was drawn, a repeated phrase or anything that might be gleaned by listening closely.

As the choir members got better at listening, my questions got harder. I might ask for the three-point outline that served as the framework of a sermon. The details became minute. It was really fun. If I forgot to quiz them, they would remind me. If I remembered wrongly, I would be quickly corrected. One of the unanticipated benefits was how these young people began to anticipate questions I might ask.

I always tried to ask at least one question that centered on the sermon's main point. During the sermon, teenage heads would turn and look at me at strategic times to see whether I was writing a question for the next test. I wore a poker face. Sometimes when I asked the questions at practice, screams of joy erupted: "I knew it! I knew it! I knew you'd ask us that!"

However, all this teen attention didn't come without an initial bribe. Any choir member who got all three questions perfectly correct (and I grade tough) got a piece of candy or a small item that was considered desirable for teens. They were not short of ideas for the rewards. After a short time, it was rare for anyone *not* to earn the reward unless they were not at worship. And worship attendance for some actually improved.

Tests such as those I gave the Atomic Praise can be given by any parent to older children and teens to help them learn to pay attention. The rewards can vary. If a family habitually goes out to eat after worship, the high scorer may pick the place. A special privilege or treat can be offered.

After a time, the reward will most likely be unnecessary. Learning to listen has its own reward. Chad and teens like him learn that they can understand a sermon, and they won't mind at all.

New Rules for a New Couch

Not all kids are as amiable as the sophomore and seven-year-old mentioned above. And I'm sure their parents can testify that they have had less-than-cooperative moments. It's not easy to change the rules with kids. It's not easy to enforce the rules either. But parents do it all the time. We create new rules and make the effort to enforce them when an issue is important to us. So take heart if you didn't get an early start in training your children to worship.

Think about a time you bought (or longed to buy) a new couch or a new car. There were few rules for the old couch. You could lie on it any old way. You could drink grape juice and read the morning paper while sitting on its old cushions. An old car? Zip through the drive-thru for burgers and fries. Wipe up what you spill; no big deal.

But a new couch? A new car? New rules. No eating food on the new couch. Take your shoes off before putting your feet up. And the no-bouncing rule that was always in effect will now be enforced. And a new car? Forget the drive-thru for the first thousand miles. Now, kids may grumble and the whole family may need reminders, but everyone adjusts to consistent en-forcement, and this means that the new car and couch stay new longer.

Your kids may grumble about worship training. The whole family will have to work at commitment, but everyone will adjust, and the new way of "going to church" will soon become the best way of actually going to *worship.*

Sermons, the Lord's Prayer, doxologies and creeds are fa-miliar parts of many services of worship. Doing old things with a new attitude gives refreshing life and deeper meaning to our habits of faith.

Young children learn the reasons behind ritual as they mem-orize the words. Older children confirm their identity in the family of God by sharing fully in the historical recitals that

define what we believe. Teens learn that sermons contain old
truth for today's world.

It is not easy for some families to do old things in a new way.
A rebellious and disinterested teen needs honesty and encouragement. Parents need to give rewards for cooperation and express their appreciation, not just their expectations. "I want to
let you know how thankful I am to have the whole family
sitting together this Sunday. Worship with you means a whole
lot to me"—such words can say a lot to a disgruntled teen. He
or she may not let you know right away, but your appreciation
is important.

New couches and new cars will be old someday, but our relationship with God will not. Scripture tells us that God's faithfulness never fails, and his mercies are new every morning. Our
children will be old someday. But new rules can help them hear
the faithfulness and mercy of God that will last forever.

saving up for something special

"**P**G" and "PG-13" are signals in our movie-going culture that parents need to be involved in selecting entertainment for children. Parental guidance provides necessary oversight and wisdom in decisions that directly affect children. As the significance of a decision increases, the guidance given by parents becomes more important accordingly.

A teenager's visit to a used-car lot needs to be a PG experience. Toddlers' viewing of Saturday-morning cartoons needs to be a PG experience. Invitations to a sleepover (these used to be called slumber parties) for grade-schoolers need to be PG experiences. Parental guidance is needed for car buying, TV watching and friend selecting. Parenting in the pew, training children to worship, is a marathon PG experience too. And it is never more important than when it concerns the sacraments of the church.

Denominational theology and congregational tradition will determine, to a significant degree, the timing and style of sacramental participation. I don't intend to discuss denominational distinctions that are argued and defended by brother and sister Christians around the world. But I *will* argue that it's very important that children recognize the extra-special significance of the biblical expressions of belief exemplified in the sacraments.

The sacraments of the faith are extra-special reenactments of what Christians believe. (The term *ordinance* is used in faith communities as expressions of faith, but for the sake of this book, I will use the word *sacrament* broadly.) Regardless of denominational distinctions, the sacraments are serious. Whether one holds to symbol or to substance, the sacredness of sacraments needs to be communicated to children.

Scraps of red, white and blue fabric are not special until they are sewn together to become the national flag. As the flag, it is protected by laws and regulations for its use and care. A flag is no longer just red, white and blue fabric. Once made into a flag, the red, white and blue fabric is not appropriately used as a tablecloth or a bedspread.

Sacraments are symbols: water, bread, juice or wine. But they are not *just* symbols. They have been made sacred and special for use in the church to help us remember and rehearse the salvation of God. The sacred nature of these common elements in the ritual of the church comes from the Word of God that once more chooses to be made visible among us "full of grace and truth" (John 1:14). We need to help our children participate in these sacraments with reverence and joy.

Baptism

Baptism is a symbol of cleansing and inclusion. The need to be cleansed from sin and initiated into the family of God is based on doctrinal tenets of Jewish-Christian heritage. God's people participate in the reenactment of Jesus' baptism in hopeful anticipation of salvation through the gift of faith or in grateful recognition of salvation through the gift of faith. However, it's important to remember that salvation itself is accomplished only through the work of Christ Jesus, his suffering, death, resurrection and ascension. It is not our experience of faith (or sacrament) that saves us, only the Savior himself. Salvation for all Christians is won in the suffering of Calvary and the resurrection of Jesus on that first Easter.

Some faith communities only baptize believers and others baptize infants or young children of Christian parents as well as those who have come to faith in Christ later in life (older children and adults) who have not been baptized. Both patterns are certainly biblical and the "when" or "how" are not central to the issue of parents having to faithfully "train up a child in the way" of Jesus Christ.

Infant baptism can be viewed as a parallel to Israel's rite of circumcision, recognizing God's promise to his children and children's children in covenantal faith. Of course, many faith communities baptize children after their own confession of faith and not as infants. In this very common and biblical practice, infants or young children are welcomed into the community and "dedicated" to the Lord. For the purpose of this book, I will use the term *baptism* to include both rites understood either as a sacrament or a dedication.

As parents, we must take our vows at the time of an infant's baptism or dedication with utmost integrity. These promises may be made on behalf of the infant in faith, or we may be promising to train the child in the faith. Talking with the pastor about the meaning of infant baptism in the denominational or congregational tradition of the family can be very helpful to parents who wish to understand and honor baptismal commitments. No matter the practice, raising a child in the community of God's people to nurture faith and understanding in our children until they acknowledge the salvation of Jesus Christ

for them in his death and resurrection is of central importance
to both parents and congregations.

In any case, as children grow older, they will begin to see the
baptism of others in the congregation. Parents can use these
occasions to teach children the significance of their own
baptism. Most children are curious about how they looked or
what they did as infants. They like to hear stories about themselves in a time that they cannot remember. Baptism can be a
profound reminder to a child about who he or she is in the
family of God.

When adults or children are baptized in a congregation,
parents can help their children understand the significance of
the event. If the children were baptized as infants, they can be
reminded of "the day this happened to you." After worship,
baptismal clothing can be brought out and pictures of the event
shown. The story of the day they were baptized can be told and
retold. This in itself is an ancient tradition of our faith.

> Hear, O Israel: The LORD our God, the LORD is one. Love
> the LORD your God with all your heart and with all your
> soul and with all your strength. These commandments
> that I give you today are to be on your hearts. Impress
> them on your children. Talk about them when you sit at
> home and when you walk along the road, when you lie
> down and when you get up. (Deuteronomy 6:4-7)

Commandments, history and the stories of redemption were
all meant to be told and retold from generation to generation in
the family of God. Sacramental rituals in the church can be the
generational bonds that help children relate to the truths of
God they need to embrace within the body of Christ. One definition of a sacrament is "a visible sign of invisible grace."
Talking about the meaning of the baptismal sacrament can help

children gain a picture of God's love and of his provision of care for and acceptance of his children.

Adult baptism is often an adolescent experience. Teens want to be accepted by the church and by God. The turbulence of the teenage years prompts many to seek repentance and the chance to "start over." So help your older children think through what it means to be baptized. You can facilitate discussions with the pastor and make sure your son or daughter can attend instructional sessions on the sacrament. Help foster an appropriate sense of seriousness concerning the decision. Teenagers are easily distracted by many things. Cars, clothes, the opposite sex, sports and schoolwork vie for priority consideration in the daily life of a teen. But you can help your teen keep priorities straight, modify schedules and put first things first. As a parent, you can *help*. But you cannot *do* the right things for your adolescent child.

Adult baptism is a decision made by the gift of grace; it must be made by the individual, in submission to the authority of the church, and with the oversight of the pastor and elders. You need to help your teen think through the motivation for his or her desire to be baptized. Make sure he or she understands that baptism is *not* something done automatically at a certain age. Try to help teens discern whether they are seeking baptism because of peer pressure or the expectations of others or because they have come to a moment of yielding to the lordship of Christ Jesus in their lives. It is the baptism of Jesus, not our own baptism, that "fulfill[s] all righteousness" (Matthew 3:15).

The Lord's Supper

Jesus instituted the sacrament of Communion to help us remember the sacrifice that made possible our reconciliation to God and to anticipate the coming of God's kingdom in its fullness. The Lord's Supper is an intimate expression of our need for God's life to be our life. Doctrinally and historically, it is the most significant confession of Christ Jesus as Lord and Savior. As the Lord's Supper was instituted in a community of believers, it also helps us become more aware of our unity in the body of Christ.

The Gospels of Matthew, Mark and Luke tell of the last meal Jesus ate with his disciples on the night of his arrest. Jesus took the symbols of the Passover meal and used them to explain a redemption that was even greater than that which saved Hebrew believers from death before their exodus from Egypt. The apostle Paul summarized the institution of the sacred meal this way:

> For I received from the Lord what I also passed on to you: The Lord Jesus, on the night he was betrayed, took bread, and when he had given thanks, he broke it and said, "This is my body, which is for you; do this in remembrance of me." In the same way, after supper he took the cup, saying, "This cup is the new covenant in my blood; do this, whenever you drink it, in remembrance of me." For whenever you eat this bread and drink this cup, you proclaim the Lord's death until he comes. (1 Corinthians 11:23-26)

Paul continued in this passage to explain the serious nature of this sacrament of remembrance. He warned against eating the bread or drinking the cup of the Lord in "an unworthy manner," and said that those who commune must "examine" themselves before they eat the bread and drink the cup (see vv. 27-30).

With this admonition in mind, taking the Lord's Supper is a serious reenactment of God's goodness and grace. The Scriptures encourage Christians to approach the table of the Lord with earnest self-examination, confession and a humble and grateful heart.

This is certainly an area of parenting that requires wisdom and oversight for one's children. Not all parents agree with my strategy for training children regarding the Lord's Supper. But I hope that this discussion will encourage parents to be very careful and thoughtful in how they help their children either prepare for or participate in this sacrament of the church.

Anticipation

The fact that a young person can explain "where babies come from" doesn't mean that he or she is ready to become a parent. Knowing the mechanical how-to of sex does not qualify a person for the responsibilities of an intimate relationship. Time, training and testing are needed before one is prepared for sexual responsibility.

The sacramental responsibility of partaking of the Lord's Supper, as laid out in Scripture, is just as serious. Young children may be able to recite John 3:16 and believe it with all their heart, but this doesn't mean they are ready for the responsibility and self-examination that comes with this sacramental expression of faith. Of course, if we all had to wait until we fully understood the mystery of faith and grace within this sacrament, none of us would come to the table. This issue isn't "how much is enough" when it comes to understanding; it's an issue of being mature enough not to need a "booster seat" to participate in the meal.

Anticipation is the best preparation for appreciation. It is good for children to wait for what is truly important. In American culture, fifteen-year-olds count down the days for the automotive rite of passage. Advent calendars help children wait and watch for Christmas. Christian parents teach their

children that waiting until marriage for sex can provide the
security needed for its full enjoyment and fulfillment.

Some faith communities give grapes or little sips to children
during Communion so they do not feel left out. I think this
may be unwise. Every day, parents deny their children experiences that are beyond a child's capacity to appreciate or handle
well. A six-year-old does not get to drive a car just because his
sixteen-year-old sister can. A three-year-old does not go to kindergarten with her five-year-old sibling, no matter how badly
she fusses about being left out. The sacred must be treated with
at least the same amount of care and oversight for the welfare of
the child.

It is traditional in some churches to allow even very young
children to take Communion. Although it is certainly possible
to help children grow to appreciate what is already theirs, it is
more difficult. Familiarity may not breed contempt in this situation, but it certainly can dull an appreciation for what should
be special.

Christian parents need to help children anticipate the joys of
participating in the supper of the Lord. The guideline for our
home was this: when Robert and Scott were able to give their
own testimony of faith before the congregation, they were old
enough to be responsible to participate in Communion with
God's people. It seems reasonable to us that when young people
are able to share clearly with others *in their own words* what
they believe regarding faith in the saving work of Jesus Christ,
then they are old enough to share in the meal the Lord gave to
his community of believers.

When our children were quite young, they could explain the
basic elements of the gospel. They had genuine experiences of
salvation when they asked Jesus to forgive their rebellion and
enter their lives. Our children had an assurance of God's

presence in their lives through some painful experiences. At an early age, they began asking to take Communion. They longed to participate.

Our response was always the same: "Are you ready to write out what you believe about Jesus and give this testimony to the church family during worship?" When they were very young the answer to both questions was "No, not yet" or "Do I have to?" to the second. It was intimidating for them to think about speaking alone in front of the whole church. For us, this was a valid sign that they were still not quite mature or prepared enough to stand on their own to participate with the congregation in sharing the Lord's Supper.

Finally, Robert and Scott were able to say yes to both questions with a measure of confidence and maturity that indicated they were in fact ready to stand on their own in the community of God's people.

Preparation

What a joy it was to read what they wrote about their faith! And it was a blessing to hear their confession of faith spoken from their hearts before the Lord and his people in worship. It was not that they had reached a certain chronological age, but that they had attained a level of spiritual and *social* maturity. Participation in the Lord's Supper requires both of these dimensions.

A young person should enter into communion with God's people on his own two feet. We did not write our children's testimonies. Robert and Scott did not memorize and recite anything that had been written by others.

Communicant classes determined by age alone do not necessarily measure individual faith, understanding or even social maturity. Innocent, enthusiastic desire is not a proper indicator of spiritual readiness for participating in the Lord's Supper.

The indicators we used were commitment, cost, personal initiative and follow-through. Given the personalities and opportunities of other families' worship situations and practices, as well as particulars in denominational theology, you may choose different indicators as you prepare your children for this sacred experience.

Think this through with your family, study the significance of the Lord's Supper in your faith tradition, talk to your pastor, and help your children share in this covenant with great seriousness. Setting this table for us cost God the life of his only Son.

If your children feel left out, neglected or deprived because they can't participate in the sacrament, it may be because explanations have been given in terms of denial, not anticipation. "No, you can't" is very different from "Not yet; it's important to wait." Parents should communicate a longing for their children to participate: "Oh, I can hardly wait until you're old enough!"

Delay is not denial. Waiting for the proper time is not idle waiting, nor is it empty. Anticipation is the best preparation for the proper moment of fulfillment. It is wise to work up a good appetite for the most significant meal in which any of us ever partake.

Practice

Because the price of this sacred meal is so high, children need to begin yearning for its taste at an early age. Whether Communion elements are given in the pew or at the front of the sanctuary in your church, your children can share the experience vicariously by just being with you.

As we sat in the pew, or when we knelt at a prayer rail, I would hold the bread and cup in my hands. I had each of the boys cup his hands around mine. With each element I would whisper the mystery of meaning in these sacred symbols as we contemplated them together. Then I took in the elements of bread and cup. Immediately, I would again hold their hands and tell them that God's love was extended to them in a special way through Jesus' death and resurrection. They were drawn into this remembrance with me.

When the boys were toddlers, my explanation sounded something like this: "This is to remind us of how Jesus had to be hurt and broken to forgive us for all we do wrong." Or I would remind them of a time during the week when they had been hurt. "Do you remember when you cut your finger this week? It hurt a lot, huh? It hurt Jesus way more than that when he died on the cross for us." Always it was a time to do what Jesus commanded when he instituted the supper. "Wow, God sure does love us. We need to be very thankful that Jesus gave his life for us."

In the Lord's Supper we celebrate the final words of Jesus' institution of the sacrament: "I tell you, I will not drink of this fruit of the vine from now on until that day when I drink it new with you in my Father's kingdom" (Matthew 26:29). The celebration of salvation from sin is a celebration of being saved for our heavenly home. Jesus is not dead, but alive. He has gone ahead of us to prepare a place for us. The Communion table is a table of preparation for a coming banquet of joy and fulfillment.

Children love parties, and this sacrament is a reminder that our God is a God of joy and celebration. And someday we will celebrate with God the victory over death and sin and lostness, won for us by "the Lamb who was slain."

I am sure that my toddlers did not understand all of this truth on a theological level, but for many years they grew into the mystery through this sacrament of reenactment. They knew by my tears, the gravity of my voice and the persistence of the message that this was a profoundly significant event. They knew by my joy in being set free to start over that Communion was a celebration of being loved by God.

As the boys grew up, explanations deepened. "To think of how much God loved us . . . how much it cost Jesus to be obedient unto death just to save us . . . what it must have meant for God to take our sin, hurt—all the bad stuff—and place it on his perfect Son . . . " Little by little the message, the elements, the symbolism and the implications for the boys' own faith took root. As they grew older, I began to see an increasingly serious mood and manner in them during the service of the sacrament. They would touch the elements reverently, and their sense of awe for this ultimate gift would be evident. Joy deepened; resting in God's secure love brought great peace.

In our congregation, whenever we take Communion together, we say "This is Christ's body, broken for you," and then "This is the blood of Christ, shed for you" as we serve each other the sacramental bread and cup. It's important that we know what we mean through this participation. For our family, building anticipation for this sacrament has been well worth the wait. When I look at Robert and Scott, who are now both taller than I am, I know this is not a sacrifice they take for granted as they serve me.

Setting an Example

Our boys were also very aware of the times when I made the decision not to participate in the Lord's Supper during a service of worship. They knew when I examined my life and knew things were not right between me, God and others. They knew about the time of pain after the murder of a dear friend. I was hurt and angry and needed to sort things out with God first. They knew about the time I was wrestling with resentment after a difficult time with people or particular situations.

In these situations, I had to remind the boys of Paul's admonition not to take Communion unworthily. I had to refrain until I could work things through in prayer with the Lord. And my children saw that God's grace was always sufficient to restore me through Scripture, prayer, repentance, confession and reconciliation. My children have seen what it means to take sin seriously. They have also seen what it means to take the grace of God seriously.

The redemption offered by Jesus in his death and remembered at Communion cannot be taken lightly. When Rob and Scott saw that I could return to the holy table full of joy, they learned that they could too. When my sons sensed my anticipation of the heavenly banquet in the kingdom of God, they began to long for this celebration too.

There are many things in life worth waiting for. I look forward to the day I drink "this fruit of the vine" in the kingdom of my Savior. And I am grateful that my children look forward to the same party and that we get to begin to anticipate that celebration now.

10

the holy hug

People often choose churches in the same way they pick dry cleaners. Do they do it the way I like it? Is there just enough starch to make it crisp but not uncomfortable? Are the creases straight? Do they spot-clean well? Do they do alterations? Are they conveniently located and reasonable in cost?

Church selection is a matter of personal preference. The decision is often based on how a congregation matches up with what one likes. Music, sermon length, preaching style, congregational demographics, sanctuary decor, dress code, denomination and the greeters' degree of friendliness are factors in the church-shopping process.

People attend church to feel better, please parents, maintain a healthy habit, set a good example, fulfill a role, get help with a problem, learn about the Bible, pray with others, teach children values, keep kids busy—and to be baptized, married and buried.

But all this is not enough for a lifetime of faith. All of the things that attract you can change. Churches and dry cleaners can go through management overhauls that make you wonder why you ever went there in the first place.

The Next Generation—Therapeutic Moral Deists or Christian Disciples?

In 2009, Oxford University Press published a book titled *Soul Searching: The Religious and Spiritual Lives of American Teenagers*. It was written by two researchers, Christian Smith and Melina Lundquist Denton, who surveyed over three thousand American teenagers who identified themselves, in a variety of descriptions, as essentially evangelical Christians. They followed up this survey with a critical mass of one-on-one interviews.

In short, what they reported was that evangelical young people understand the Christian faith as "therapeutic moral deists." "Therapeutic" because believing in God made them feel generally better about themselves. Jesus was good for their self-esteem. "Moral" because their faith helped them know right from wrong behaviors and kept them out of trouble. And "deists" because this God, other than offering these interior props to life, really didn't have much to do with their day-to-day lives. Now, this is an extremely barebones summary of research that caused more than a few congregational leaders to rethink and rework their ministry to youth.

None of Denton and Smith's research results surprised me. It confirmed what I had been trying to counter in my work with parenting in the pew for years. Worship designed for God's pleasure and by God's Word and mediated by God's Spirit will deal with our sin-sick lives as an honest approach to how we esteem ourselves. Worship designed for God's pleasure and by God's Word and mediated by God's Spirit will expose the need for the imputed righteousness of Christ Jesus that goes much deeper than our behaviors, which are only a symptom, an evidence, of the state of our human nature. Worship designed for God's pleasure and by God's Word and mediated by God's Spirit brings us face to face with the God who shapes us in the sanctuary to send us into the real world.

The intergenerational nature of the church is vitally important to God and needs to be nurtured in our worship, programs, mission and community life. Too many congregations follow the highly successful marketing strategy of our culture. Specialty stores for every age. Gap and Baby Gap. What middle-aged woman doesn't love Coldwater Creek clothes because they disguise our hips? So we give the teens at church a youth house across the street; the old people have their own study groups; and we keep children out of the sanctuary. We provide style-shaped options for worship services so the hip can have a praise band and the aged can hold a hymnbook and sing with a well-played pipe organ.

Then we wonder why those in the next generation just wander off "somewhere" and complain that they didn't feel like they belonged. Well, maybe they never really did. All through their childhood and teen years they belonged to *their* group, not to the congregation, the church itself. The same "my group" mentality and practice is often extended in their college experience. It's often after college when these church kids discover they have no place to belong anymore. So they either give up looking for just the right community that suits them (continuing the process begun with ecclesial niche marketing) or they wander away from a faith that only shaped them to be therapeutic moral deists.

It takes the church to make disciples. Intentional intergenerational development within a church is hard in our culture because it is countercultural. It's hard because it's biblical. It's hard because it's costly—everyone in the congregation has to die to themselves to be servants to one another under the headship of Christ Jesus. As many parents have said a million times to their children, "If it's not hard, it's not worth it."

Intergenerational communities making disciples of all ages are simply worth it. Old people need the fresh laughter and perplexing humor of teenagers. Teenagers need to hear stories of faith and perseverance that number more years than they have lived. Single parents need to be included in unfractured families, and blended families need the inclusion of "aunts" and "uncles" in a fiduciary family that is less complicated than their own.

It takes work to figure out how to include children in small groups, teens in potluck suppers and children in worship. The apostle Paul celebrated the work and declared the effort worth it because in Christ "there is neither Jew nor Gentile, neither slave nor free, nor is there male and female" (Galatians 3:28). In the body of Christ there is no room for racism, socioeconomic prejudice or sexism. And there is no room for chronological snobbery. As Paul wrote at the conclusion of his famous trilogy in Galatians, "For you are all one in Christ Jesus. If you belong to Christ, then you are Abraham's seed, and heirs according to the promise" (Galatians 3:28-29).

Only God, revealed in Jesus Christ, is "the same yesterday and today and forever" (Hebrews 13:8). Only in God can we find hope. Only when we learn to worship, rather than just go to church, will we be at rest. Only God offers stability in our rapidly changing and decaying world.

Worship is a gem of truth in a marketplace of cheap imitations. Encountering God is meeting the Reality that undergirds all of life. When we introduce our children to what is completely genuine, we are equipping them to judge all the other experiences and possibilities that will come to them.

Many young people today wonder whether there is anything certain, anyone they can completely trust. Traditions, whether family, country or faith, are not automatically embraced. Our children are growing up in a time when religious hypocrisy is declining. Few people are just-Christmas-and-Easter, nominal Christians. In many respects, evil is more openly evil; people are less embarrassed by lapses in common morality. Few young people will continue participation in congregational faith communities out of habit or family tradition.

Great numbers of young people are growing up in the spiritual vacuum created by the exclusion of God from home and society. People are increasingly suspicious of being manipulated by those who popularly franchise religious experience. The only One who can completely fill the spiritual vacuum is God revealed in Jesus Christ. And like Augustine's heart sixteen centuries ago, the hearts of our children are restless.

The rest of God remains for those who enter into God's presence and receive his mercy and grace to help in times of need (Hebrews 4:9-16). Worship teaches us how to enter into God's rest—to cease striving and to know the One who saves us (Psalm 46:10).

Children need to rest these days. Even so, much of their recreation is competition, strife and performance. Few children are "re-created" by sports. Winning gives the only momentary joy. Losing, failing or coming in second robs many children of any enjoyment, even in the effort. (And even if no official score is kept, kids know who "won.")

Parents, too, need to rest these days. The gospel of Jesus Christ gives us the freedom to fail. The Lord of life has come to call not the righteous but sinners to repentance. This is very good news to me. I rejoice that Jesus loves me. I can be honest with him about the difficulties, disappointments and sin in my life. He will not turn away.

Parenting is much harder than I thought it would be. And parenting in the pew may be the hardest parenting of all. I have failed more than I thought I ever would. I have done some really stupid things as a mother, even at worship. I have felt things that I didn't think real mothers could feel about their offspring. But always I could go to Jesus. Always his mercy was new every morning. His faithfulness is indeed great.

And I could go to the boys and own up to my lack of wisdom, my shortcomings, my failure. And, just as with the Lord, it was no surprise to them. My children have forgiven me many times.

This capacity to weather the storms of child rearing came in significant measure because of our "oasis" of rest and reminder. The pew has been a place of love for us. We have rested with each other. I think we could rest like this because we were aware of being in the presence of a perfect Parent. Our Father was watching over us.

It's vitally important to realize that not only is God watchful in worship, but through the Son and by the Spirit, God is also the mediator of worship. Believers who gather for worship don't invoke the presence of God; they respond to the God who calls them to worship. Worship is a time of remembrance to us because our Father meets us there and shows us the way back home. Over and over again God meets us and reminds us of his love and mercy. We have been reminded Sunday after Sunday that he knows it all and loves us still.

Through worshiping together, my children and I have become pilgrims journeying boldly to the throne of grace. As fellow sinners, we follow our "high priest" Jesus "behind the curtain" to worship our Father by the mediation of the Spirit (Hebrews 4:14-16). In worship we have learned to love God and accept his mercy. In worship we have learned to love each other, accept our failures and practice forgiveness.

God must be real in our experience of faith. He must be known and encountered. We cannot be satisfied with worship that simply fulfills social and religious obligations. God must be heard. We need to teach our children what it means to touch the hem of his garment and be healed. Our children need to clamber into the loving lap of the Savior. Jesus still yearns for the companionship of children and longs to bless them.

If Sunday becomes a holy joy for us, what joy the Father must know as Jesus, our great mediator and high priest, presents us before the throne of grace through the real presence of the Holy Spirit (Hebrews 4:14-17)! This is the Christian life, and worship is the time and place where we celebrate this reality with the family of God. As Jesus said, "Let the little children come to me, and do not hinder them, for the kingdom of God belongs to such as these" (Mark 10:14).

Parenting in the pew is a response to Jesus' admonition not to hinder our children. It is one way to take our children by the hand and guide them to the embrace and blessing of the Savior. Teaching your children to worship is helping them learn to give the Lord a holy hug—to bless him with the embrace of their souls.

I remember how, when the boys were quite small, they would bring me their "writing"—jagged scribbles on scraps of paper— and I would display it on the refrigerator. And it occurs to me that worship is a time when I bring the scribbles of my life and my Father puts them on his heavenly refrigerator—all the scribbles, not just the pretty ones or the ones that make sense. He is the perfect Parent who always sees what's really there. This is the Father of truth and grace I wanted my children to know and love.

I watched my sons through the years bring their scribbles— the struggles and joys of their life with God—to worship. As I saw their scribbles placed on our Father's refrigerator, I began to see who my sons really are. Sitting beside me was the handwork of God. And God, who began a good work in them, promised to bring them to maturity in Christ in the perfection of time (Philippians 1:6). In the presence of our Father, my sons have become my brothers. There is no greater joy for any parent in the pew.

May *Parenting in the Pew* lead you and your congregation to explore more and more the wonder of belonging together in Christ who is our head. And may our children and grandchildren become disciples of Jesus in our midst—indeed, our brothers and sisters who join us in the worship, witness, mission and community of the church.

thank you

It has been an exercise in gratitude to put on paper how good God has been to me as a parent in the pew. The living and now the writing of this book have taken nearly half of my life. My life has been and is a life inundated by the grace of God. I can trace his goodness in those he has sent to love me and encourage me along the way.

I am very thankful for my parents and sister, who have come alongside me to share the life of faith in Christ. I give thanks for Jennings and Marjorie Lee, who first opened the door to the church for our family. Unknown even to them, the hope and healing of our family began at that time.

My friend and mentor as a pastor's wife, Betty Henderson, told me not to "judge October apples in June" and modeled patience in motherhood that I needed to see.

Clara Kendrick prayed for me as I wrote and encouraged me to be faithful. Andy Le Peau at InterVarsity Press heard my passion for worship through a very rough draft and first suggested that I write for parents. I am grateful for his insight and for the expertise Rodney Clapp shared to finish what was started for the first edition. My thanks extend to Cindy Bunch, the editor of this third edition and, again, to Andy Le Peau, who wanted a new generation to think through the encouragement and help parents today in training children in worship for a lifetime of Christian discipleship.

And, of course, my husband, Breck, and sons Robert and Scott are due my fondest expressions of gratitude. Breck is my pastor and dearest friend. I could sit in any pew if he was in the pulpit. Rob and Scott are my friends as well as my children. Our story is a gift of God's goodness to us as we learned to worship side by side. And our story continues now with a new generation of disciples. The joy of seeing God's faithful work in our children's children is beyond description.

And special thanks to our Carolyn Park church family. *Parenting in the Pew* was first written in your pews, first "read" by your eyes. Thank you for loving Robert and Scott. Thank you for loving Mom and Dad too. And to all the congregations I've visited and parents I've met since the first publication of *Parenting in the Pew*, thank you for sharing your children with me. May you continue to know the wonder of seeing sons and daughters become brothers and sisters in Christ for generations to come.

discussion questions
and reflections

You might want to a ten-week Sunday school class or home study group to read *Parenting in the Pew* together and then discuss what works, what is challenging and what new tools can help children worship within the context of your congregational worship. We need to help cheer each other on in this adventure of parenting children.

Consider inviting empty-nest older people who love you and your children to join you in reading and discussing the book. These extra loving hands can pray for you and your children and can even help parents (especially parents with several children or children with particular challenges) on Sunday mornings.

Chapter 1: Daddy, I'd Like You to Meet My Children

1. What makes worship with your toddler/grade-schooler/ teen most difficult? What do you find most distracting?

2. Reflect personally or share with the group your memories of church in your childhood. What are your most endearing memories? Did you have any regrettable experiences or times that were dreaded?

3. If you were to invite an interested but unchurched person

to worship with your congregation, how would you describe your church and service?

4. Identify both the things that help you and the things that hinder you from "preparing for worship" in contrast to just "going to church." Brainstorm ways parents in your congregation can help each other learn to worship as an intergenerational community of faith and value the contributions of a wide variety of people of different ages and life situations in the congregation. How can you help children express their respect of and appreciation for others in worship?

Scripture Reflection: Psalm 96
Read the entire psalm aloud for personal reflection or as a study group.

> Ascribe to the LORD, all you families of nations,
>   ascribe to the LORD glory and strength.
> Ascribe to the LORD the glory due his name;
>   bring offerings and come into his courts. (vv. 7-8)

How does your family "give" to the Lord in worship? What family and church traditions provide opportunities for your child(ren) to be a part of giving to the Lord?

Pray for the pastor, worship leaders, parents and children in your congregation.

Chapter 2: Worship BC and AD

1. Why is worship important to your personal life of faith in Jesus? What do you consider most meaningful to you in a service of worship?

2. Reflect on a time when God's presence in a worship service was particularly meaningful or life changing. What made this time poignant and memorable?

3. How has your worship *experience* changed since AD began for you? How can others in your church family help you as a parent in the pew?

Scripture Reflection: Lamentations 3:20-26
Read the entire Scripture selection aloud for personal reflection or as a study group.

> Because of the LORD's great love we are not consumed,
>> for his compassions never fail.
> They are new every morning;
>> great is your faithfulness. (vv. 22-23)

How can the faithfulness of the Lord as a patient Father encourage your own faithfulness and patience as a parent? How can the example of the Lord help you be a better "worship coach" for your child(ren)?

Pray for the pastor, worship leaders, parents and children in your congregation.

Chapter 3: Praise and Puppies

1. Reflect on times when children have had spiritual insights that helped you in your own understanding of the Lord. What things have your own children taught you about the life of faith?

2. How have you or others helped explain deep issues of life, death and the Christian faith to toddlers/grade-schoolers/teens? How did you gain an understanding of these things?

3. What can you, other parents, pastors and worship leaders do to help the congregation as a whole appreciate the value of including children in worship?

4. How does the idea of worship as service—an invitation to

work—influence your sense of needing to be more intentional about preparing for and participating in worship? (The word liturgy literally means "the work of the people.")

Scripture Reflection: Matthew 18:1-6
Read the entire Scripture selection aloud for personal reflection or as a study group.

> And whoever welcomes one such child in my name
> welcomes me. (v. 5)

How can multigenerational congregations be a special resource for families today that often live far from relatives? How can the church family help single-parent families?

Pray for your pastor and church leaders as they serve all the generations within your congregation.

Chapter 4: Sunday Morning Starts on Saturday Night

1. List ideas that will help your family begin Sunday on Saturday night. Share these with your family or study group.

2. Share ideas on how you can make Sundays simple but special for your child(ren). How have you made the Christian message central in the life of your family on special holy days like Christmas and Easter? How can you share these celebrations with the wider church family? (For instance, have a birthday party for Jesus on the Sunday before Christmas—even with a cake and candles. Have each family bring a wrapped package containing a family work of art representing the talent, burden or thank offering each member of the family gives to the Lord. These can be placed in an empty "manger.")

3. How can you continue or begin to teach generosity to your child(ren) in giving to the work and life of the church?

4. Think through what you can do to help children understand the space (sanctuary, worship center and so on) where you worship and how it is a special, set-apart space for worship. What do you think is helpful (or not) about the space where you worship?

Scripture Reflection: Psalm 84
Read the entire psalm aloud for personal reflection or as a study group.

> How lovely is your dwelling place,
>   LORD Almighty!
> My soul yearns, even faints,
>   for the courts of the LORD;
> my heart and my flesh cry out
>   for the living God. (vv. 1-2)

What occasions in your family are well planned and anticipated with enthusiasm? How can this energy and interest be cultivated in your family's preparations for weekly worship? Pray for your children and your home.

Pray for your weekly schedules, priorities and time management. Pray for your pastor, worship leaders and Sunday-school teachers.

Chapter 5: Counting Bricks or Encountering God

1. Think about the church building of your childhood. What do you remember about the sanctuary? What distractions do you recall? What were the expectations of your parents, and how were they communicated?

2. Discuss the difference for children between being entertained and being invited to participate in worship. What is your congregational tradition concerning the age when

children are in the worship service for the entire time? How does your service of worship include children? (Is there a children's sermon? Are children addressed in the adult sermon? Is there music or a choir that encourages the participation of worship? Do teens have regular opportunities to help in the service or give testimonies?

3. If your church provides papers and projects for children to use in the worship service, how can you use these to make sure worship, not just a well-meant distraction, is the result? How can you use the implements and helps for worship (bulletin, hymnbook and so on) to guide your child(ren) in participating more directly in the service?

4. Who are a couple of people in your congregation that may be helpful to you as a family in the pew by praying for you regularly and/or sitting with you and supporting your efforts to engage in the service of worship?

Scripture Reflection: Ephesians 5:15-17
Read the entire Scripture selection aloud for personal reflection or as a study group.

Making the most of every opportunity. (v. 16)

Consider the investment parents make in the lives of their children. What do you consider important in the maturing and training of your child(ren)? How is your limited time each week as a parent in the pew valued by you, your child(ren) and others in the church?

Pray for yourself as you learn to train your children in the joys of worship. Pray for your relationship with the Lord to be enriched by this use of your time and energy. Pray for other parents in your church and for your pastor and worship leaders.

Chapter 6: Make a Joyful Noise

1. How would you describe the music used in the worship service of your congregation? How does music influence your own worship of the Lord?

2. What role does music in general play in the life of your toddler/grade-schooler/teen? How can you help your child worship through the music opportunities in the liturgy of your congregation?

3. Discuss with your family or study group the various ways music can be used in the home to train for worship. Consider not only music in which the congregation participates but also music that is offered to God by choirs and musicians in worship.

4. Select a hymn or praise song used fairly often in your congregational service of worship, and think through how you would explain its meaning to your young child or discuss its meaning with a teen.

Scripture Reflection: Psalm 148
Read the entire psalm aloud for personal reflection or as a study group.

> Young men and women,
>> old men and children.
> Let them praise the name of the Lord,
>> for his name alone is exalted;
> his splendor is above the earth and the heavens. (vv. 12-13)

This psalm reflects how all of creation is commanded to offer praise to the Lord. How can music be used at home and at church to facilitate the praise of God? How can music be misused and become a distraction in the worship of God?

Pray for the choir director(s) and those involved in the music ministry of your congregation. Pray for your pastor. Pray for your family and the use of music in your home to give praise and honor to the Lord.

Chapter 7: Prayer, Confession and Canned Goods

1. What do you remember about prayer from your childhood? Who taught you to pray, and how did you learn to pray?

2. Think about various ways you can teach your toddler/ grade-schooler/teen to pray. Share these ideas with your family or study group. Discuss the importance of modeling prayer both at home and in the congregational worship.

3. What opportunities for prayer are offered in the worship service of your congregation? Some prayers are led by the worship leader or pastor; some may be prayed in unison, like the Lord's Prayer; some may be spontaneous and include the prayers of the congregation; some may be in silence. In each of these, how can children be helped to participate and learn to pray?

4. Think about the ABCs of congregational prayer: audible, brief, Christ-centered. If your service of worship has a time when the congregation prays aloud, how might you help a child prepare at home to participate in this moment during worship?

Scripture Reflection: Matthew 6:8-13
Read the entire Scripture selection aloud for personal reflection or as a study group.

Our Father . . .

Think through how you would help explain the meaning of each phrase of this model prayer (used by Jesus to train the disciples how to pray) to your toddler/grade-schooler/teen. How can this prayer help you pray for your child(ren)?

Use this Scripture outline to pray for your child(ren), yourself and your pastor.

Chapter 8: Just How Long Was That Sermon?

1. How would you describe the sermon style of your pastor? Think about how Scripture is explained, illustrated and applied within the sermon. How do you think the sermon contributes to the worship of God as well as to the teaching and training of the congregation?

2. Think about any difficulties you experience during the sermon in helping your toddler/grade-schooler/teen to listen and learn. Share these with your family or study group. Also share ideas that may be helpful to you and other parents in training children to learn from God's Word.

3. How can a children's sermon be used in your congregation's service of worship to help children listen to the adult sermon? How can a teaching time directed at children be used to train them in understanding other parts of a service of worship?

4. Share creative ideas for ways to discuss the scriptural text(s) and sermon for families with older children.

Scripture Reflection: Romans 10:13-17
Read the entire Scripture selection for personal reflection or as a study group.

> How can they hear without someone preaching to them?
> . . . Faith comes from hearing the message, and the message is heard through the word about Christ. (vv. 14, 17)

How does the sermon affect your spiritual growth in Christ? What can you do in a service of worship to better "hear" the preached Word? Consider things like participation in an act of response in the service itself, the use of the Bible during the sermon, application of the preached word, accountability to "do" the word and not be a "hearer only," etc. Then consider how to help children at age-appropriate times participate in the things you've found helpful.

How can personal or small-group study of Scripture during the week help you learn the Word of God? How can the daily hearing of Scripture in the home help your children live a life of faith?

Pray for your pastor as he or she prepares the sermon for the congregation. Pray for your family to have listening ears and teachable hearts to learn the Word of God.

Chapter 9: Saving Up for Something Special

1. Summarize the practice of sacraments or ordinances in your congregation. How are children introduced to this aspect of life of the church? What help or instruction does your pastor or Christian education resources provide for your family in these practices?

2. What can you do to help your child(ren) prepare a testimony of faith to be shared with others throughout life? How do you summarize the gospel truths in language understandable to your toddler/grade-schooler/teen? Work on this with your family or study group.

3. How can you help your children appreciate the sacraments of the church while they wait and observe others within the congregation? How do sacraments contribute to the worship of God in your church?

4. Talk with your pastor or children's ministry director about giving *Parenting in the Pew* to parents when children are baptized or dedicated in your congregation. This can be one way to help equip young parents to keep their promises to raise their children in the light of faith in the community of God's people.

Scripture Reflection: Luke 24:25-35
Read the entire Scripture selection aloud for personal reflection or as a study group.

Jesus was recognized by them when he broke the bread. (v. 35)

How do you recognize the grace of God in the sacraments of your church? What do you do within the liturgy of your congregation to grow in your appreciation of the sacraments?

How do you explain the meaning and practice of sacraments to your toddler/grade-schooler/teen in words appropriate to his or her age and understanding? Work on this with your family or study group.

Pray for your family to be faithfully prepared for the reception of sacraments within the church. Pray for your pastor and worship leaders as they oversee the sacramental liturgy of the congregation.

Chapter 10: The Holy Hug

1. What progress and frustrations have you experienced as you have been training your child(ren) in worship? Share these with your family or study group.

2. How can others in the congregation be helpful to you as a parent in the pew? How can others in the congregation encourage your children as they learn to worship?

3. If God did have a refrigerator, what would you think about seeing your life's writing there? How do you experience the grace and mercy of God in the life of your family?

4. Discuss the "shape" of your service of worship. How does it help the congregation reenact the story of salvation? How can you help children recognize God's story reflected in the liturgy?

Scripture Reflection: Deuteronomy 4:9-10 and 2 Timothy 3:14-15
Read the entire Scripture selections aloud for personal reflection or as a study group.

Teach [these things] to your children and to their children after them. (Deuteronomy 4:9)

Continue in what you have learned and have become convinced of. . . . From infancy you have known the holy Scriptures. (2 Timothy 3:14-15)

What do you hope to achieve in the spiritual training of your child(ren)?

What do you desire for your children concerning their relationship with God by the time they are ready to have their own family?

How can your parenting efforts in the spiritual training of your children continue to mature your own relationship with God?

Pray for your children's future. Pray for yourself and other parents to trust the Lord while being faithful in the challenge and commitment to be parents in the pew. Pray for your pastor as a parent or grandparent to his or her own child(ren).

for further reading

here are a few resources especially intended for children's educators within the church to help equip parents, volunteers and other ministry staff in the development of children's ministry and the intergenerational dynamics of congregational life.

Allen, Holly Catterton, and Christine Lawton Ross. *Intergenerational Christian Formation: Bringing the Whole Church Together in Ministry, Community and Worship.* Downers Grove, Ill.: InterVarsity Press, 2012.

This book is written by two educators (Holly Allen is a university colleague of mine at John Brown University) who have worked in and taught children's ministry in the congregational setting for many years. It deals with the benefits of intergenerational communities and makes the case on broadly evangelical biblical, theological foundations as well as theoretical foundations in education. The book discusses challenges for intergenerational development in today's highly compartmentalized culture. There is also a lengthy section devoted to intergenerational practice for worship, learning, sharing, mission and small groups, as well as other topics.

Bunge, Marcia J., ed. *The Child in Christian Thought.* Grand Rapids: Eerdmans, 2001.

This book is an anthology of essays by several writers and is a comprehensive survey of the history of Christian thinking concerning the education and spiritual nature and understanding of children. The survey runs from the New Testament to contemporary communities.

Castleman, Robbie F. *Story-Shaped Worship: Following Patterns from the Bible and History.* Downers Grove, Ill.: InterVarsity Press, 2013.

This is the book that I have affectionately dubbed my grown-up version of the foundations of *Parenting in the Pew.* If you want to know more about the biblical shape of Christian worship and the dynamic of the reenactment of God's salvation that is embedded in the Old and New Testament and reflected in various ways throughout church history, you'll like this book. Thinking through what worship is, both to God and to his people, is vitally important in a culture driven by personal taste.

Dawn, Marva J. *Is It a Lost Cause? Having the Heart of God for the Church's Children.* Grand Rapids: Eerdmans, 1997.

My friend Marva has a compelling way of getting at cultural critique in both world and congregation with insight and passion. Though published in 1997, this book anticipates some of the challenges facing congregations and parents today. This is not a dated book; it is full of wisdom as well as warning.